THE
HANDBOOK
ON
HEALING

THE
HANDBOOK
ON
HEALING

COLIN
URQUHART

OLIVER
NELSON

THOMAS NELSON PUBLISHERS
Nashville • Atlanta • London • Vancouver

Published in Nashville, Tennessee, by Thomas Nelson, Inc., Publishers,
and distributed in Canada by Word Communications, Ltd., Richmond,
British Columbia.

Originally published in Great Britain by Hodder and Stoughton Limited,
Mill Road, Dunton Green, Sevenoaks, Kent TN13 2YA, England.

Scripture quotations are taken from the HOLY BIBLE, NEW INTERNA-
TIONAL VERSION®. Copyright © 1973, 1978, 1984 by International Bible
Society. Used by permission of Zondervan Publishing House. All rights
reserved.

Library of Congress Cataloging-in-Publication Data

Urquhart, Colin.
    [Receive your healing]
    The handbook on healing / Colin Urquhart.
        p.   cm.
    Originally pulished: Receive your healing. Sevenoaks, Kent,
England : Hodder and Stoughton, 1986.
    ISBN 0-7852-8342-0 (pbk.)
    1. Spiritual healing.   2. Jesus Christ—Miracles.   3. Healing in the
Bible. I. Title.
BT732.5.U76 1994
234'.13—dc20   93-48888
                                                                   CIP

Printed in the United States of America.

        1 2 3 4 5 6 — 99 98 97 96 95 94

To all who need healing
through Jesus

CONTENTS

Part Seven:
Deliverance

Part Eight:
Failure

Part Nine:
The Healing Church

Epilogue

Appendix:
Faith-Building Scriptures

ACKNOWLEDGMENTS

For several years people have been suggesting I write a book on healing. I have been reluctant to do so because this is such a vast subject with so much to learn. However, when God impresses something on you, it is right to obey.

I have endeavored to keep this book simple and to direct readers to the truth of the Scriptures that their faith may be enlarged.

My thanks are due to all who have helped me in the twenty-plus years of exercising a healing ministry. My wife has been a constant source of love, encouragement, and prayer; my children have been my children—and that is all I ask of them! Andrea has helped with the Scripture references, and Richard with the material for the testimonies used.

Last, but by no means least, my thanks to my secretary, Annette, for the countless hours of work on typewriter and word processor and for the love and devotion she has shown to the task.

||||||||||||||||||||||||||||||||||||||||||||||||

Part One

GOD'S PROVISION FOR YOUR HEALING

||||||||||||||||||||||||||||||||||||||||||||||||

DOES GOD WANT TO HEAL ME?

The building was crowded as John stood to speak. Three years previously I had been in this same city in western England to conduct a short mission. John, in an advanced stage of multiple sclerosis, had been present at one of the meetings. Already his senses and coordination were seriously affected, having had the disease for nine years, and he had long since given up his employment as a bus driver.

He recalled that God had given me a word of knowledge for someone present who had a serious disease of the central nervous system: "You know that He can heal you, but you doubt that He will." John identified immediately with that word.

The word of knowledge continued: "But despite your un-belief the Lord is beginning His healing in you now." At that moment John felt something in his feet, which had been completely numb for years. During the next three weeks, the power of God moved through his body from the soles of his feet to the top of his head, releasing every part from the dreadful effects of that disease. He was restored to normal health, and one week after the meeting he was able to go for a four-mile walk with his family. "It was a healing for the whole family," John said. "Now I could do all the normal things with my children that I had been unable to do for years."

In due course John was ready to return to his job as a bus driver. He had to undergo exhaustive medical tests before his public vehicle license could be restored, but the doctors could find no trace of the multiple sclerosis. Never before had it been known for such a license to be restored to anyone who had contracted this disease.

It is good to hear such testimonies of the way in which God is willing to heal His people today, testimonies that have stood the test of time. However, John's dilemma is one shared by many others: Does God want to heal me? Is it really His purpose to heal me? Why haven't I received all the healing I need?

Some doubt God's desire to heal; others, like John, almost give up believing because they see so little change in their circumstances.

Is it always God's purpose to heal? How can we receive His healing power? How are we able to communicate His healing power to others? How can we learn to pray with faith, confident that God will answer our prayers for healing?

Our faith will be challenged by what we see in the Scriptures. Sometimes you may want to cry out in protest that your experience does not match what God says in His Word. *He wants to raise your experience to the level of His Word, not reduce His Word to the level of your experience.*

We shall have to face honestly an inevitable question: If it is God's purpose to heal, why is not everybody healed?

BEGINNING WITH THE NATURAL

God is the Creator. *He made you to be healthy and to feel well.* You have a natural desire to be healthy, both emotionally and physically. If you experience tension, anxiety, or fear, you want to be at peace. If you have physical pain, you want to be free as soon as possible, both of the pain and of its cause. Your normal reaction to sickness is to seek a cure.

God has created you with natural healing properties that automatically function when something is wrong. If you break an arm, the natural healing processes in your body will cause the bone to grow together. A surgeon can set the bone in the correct position, but he cannot make it grow. No doctor can heal; he can only cooperate with the natural healing processes at work within the body. He may stimulate those processes through various treatments, including the use of drugs; he may aid them through surgery; but he cannot heal the wounds. His training teaches him to cooperate with the natural healing processes within the patient's body.

These things are obvious but point us to an important truth: *God, our Creator, wants us to be healthy.* When He first created male and female, what He made was good. Sickness and death only entered human experience at the time of the Fall when Adam and Eve yielded to temptation and sinned. Ever since, it has been God's purpose to restore His people to the state of wholeness or perfection in which they were first created. *He wants you to be whole, to be healthy in every way—spiritually, mentally, emotionally, and physically.*

NO COMPETITION BETWEEN GOD AND DOCTORS

There is no competition between God and doctors. If healing is God's purpose, doctors and nurses are cooperating with His divine will. The way in which they can do this is limited, whereas God is unlimited in His ability to restore what He has made. But we do not have to see a dichotomy between the medical profession and the practice of divine healing.

Many Christians who receive God's healing power supernaturally have already been under the direction of their doctors and have been helped by receiving medical attention. There are many fine Christian doctors who use their medical expertise within the context of a life of prayer and faith. Certainly, if she needs healing, a Christian's first thought should be to pray. The nonbeliever will visit his doctor without a thought given to prayer.

DOUBLE-MINDEDNESS

Some imagine that God wants them to be sick, that He is glorified in their sickness, and that this is part of His plan for their lives. Usually those who say such things are happy to consult their doctors. Yet to do so is totally inconsistent with what they profess. If God wants them to be sick and desires to be glorified in their illness, they should not seek any remedy or relief through either prayer or the medical profession; that would make doctors active agents against God's will. To seek help would be to go against what they claim to be God's purpose. To be consistent, they should suffer their pain willingly, glad to be at one with what they claim to be God's will.

Such a position is ridiculous. It is alien to the way God created us with a desire to be healthy, and it denies completely the teaching of Jesus and the New Testament.

In practice, many who say sickness is His will are happy to undergo operations and take drugs to alleviate their problem.

The matter is very simple. If God wants you to be healthy, and that is certainly His best purpose, *it is right to look to Him with faith and pray to be healed.* There can be nothing wrong with consulting medical opinion if necessary. But it is better to be healed by God with the positive side effect of your faith in Him being strengthened than to submit to the surgeon's knife or take drugs with possible negative side effects.

If God does not want you to be healed, however, there is no point in praying or exercising faith for healing or even seeking medical attention.

It is totally inconsistent for you to adopt the position that God does not want to heal you, that it is not His purpose to heal you, and at the same time seek a medical cure. If it is His purpose, He is ready to help you come to faith for your healing.

God wants you to be whole and healthy. It is always His purpose both to aid the natural healing processes in your body and to answer your prayers of faith with His supernatural power, available to all who believe and trust in Him.

> *God does not want you to be double-minded about*
>   *healing.*
> *He has made you to be healthy.*
> *When you are sick, He wants to heal you.*
> *His natural healing processes are at work in your body.*
> *His supernatural healing power is available to you.*
> *He wants to teach you how to appropriate the healing*
>   *you need.*

O LORD my God, I called to you for help and you healed me (Ps. 30:2).

2

WHAT DOES IT MEAN TO BE HEALED?

You want to be happy and emotionally healthy. You want to have loving and affectionate relationships. You want to be relieved of mental anguish, anxiety, tensions, and fears. If you are sick or in pain, you desire physical healing. You do not like pain and disease. Neither do you want to live in fear of sickness.

WHOLENESS

God wants you to be spiritually healthy as well as emotionally and physically healthy. His purpose for you is wholeness. Your emotional and physical health depend to a very large extent upon your spiritual well-being.

God's healing purposes for you are complete. He wants you to be spiritually healthy, emotionally healthy, physically healthy; He wants you to have healthy relationships, healthy attitudes, a healthy environment. He wants healthy nations and a healthy society.

To speak of all these areas of God's concern within the compass of one book is clearly impossible. We shall confine ourselves to discussing how we can receive personal healing from God, how our faith in Him should not only have spiritual consequences but also result in our emotional and physical well-being.

Through surgery and medicine, doctors can cooperate with the natural healing properties at work within us. In response to prayer, God can stimulate the natural healing processes and intervene in supernatural and miraculous ways. It is within His power to do what is naturally and medically impossible. *He is the God who made us, and He is the God who can mend us, no matter what the need.*

SIN IS SICKNESS

To be whole is to be spiritually, emotionally, and physically healthy. Jesus lived in perfect wholeness; He neither sinned nor was He ever sick. In one sense we all need healing because none of us is yet perfect like Him. Sickness is a failure to be like Jesus. He was the man who lived human life to the full. He was never sick because He never sinned; He never became tainted with the fallen nature of creation. He resisted every temptation to grieve God and disobey Him.

Some leaders of the revival happening among the aboriginal people in remote parts of Australia were asked about the welfare of a particular Christian brother. They said he was sick because he had fallen into grave sin and was not walking with the Lord. They were praying for him to be healed.

The sickness to which they referred was not physical or emotional but spiritual and moral. They have a biblical view of sickness. Sin is sickness and, unless a person repents, can often lead to physical illness.

We live in a fallen and sinful world and are tainted by the existence of sin, sickness, and disease. God wants us to resist temptation and to learn how to resist the sickness around us. When we sin, He is ready to forgive, and when we are sick, He wants to heal us—spiritually, emotionally, and physically. God sent His Son into this world to bring salvation to His people. *Salvation* means "healing" in the full sense of the word. *On the cross Jesus gave Himself—spirit, soul, and body—to bring salvation—healing of spirit, soul, and body—to those who trust in Him.*

GOD'S PURPOSE IS TO HEAL

Unless you understand that it is God's purpose to heal you when you are sick, you will find it difficult, or even impossible, to exercise faith to receive healing from Him. How can you believe God *will* heal you if you do not believe He *wants* to heal you?

Lay aside your arguments from experience and look at what the Bible says about healing; then you can learn how to relate to your experience what God says. The Scriptures demonstrate that it is God's purpose to heal, and they teach us how to receive that healing. *Healing is always God's best and finest purpose when one of His children is sick.* Ignorance and disbelief of that truth have resulted in many Christians accepting sickness as God's will for them.

Why isn't everyone healed? You can answer that question with another: Why doesn't everyone believe in Jesus? God *desires* that all receive salvation; Christ came and died for all. He did not come to condemn; He came to save. Yet clearly not all people are saved. Not everybody is brought to a saving knowledge and experience of Jesus in new birth. Not all know Jesus or put their trust in what He has done for them on the cross, a sacrifice that alone can make them acceptable to God in this life and for all eternity.

Not even God can have all that He wants because He will not compromise His justice and righteousness. He wants all people to be saved, but not all people are saved because not all believe in the means of salvation God Himself has provided. He sent His Son to bring the good news of the kingdom and to die on the cross to make it possible for people to enter His kingdom. Because of human sin and unbelief, God has to accept what is less than His best. He has provided the way of salvation for all, but He saves only those who repent of their sins and put their faith in Jesus.

Let me ask you another simple question. Do you ever sin? The answer to that is obvious. Of course you do! Does God want you to sin? No, of course He does not want that. The fact that you sin means God's best purpose for your life is not realized, for sin is whatever is contrary to God's will for you. God calls you to fulfill His plan for your life but has to take sin into account. He knows you will sin and are not yet perfect in all your ways; but this knowledge does not prevent Him from using you and working through you. He uses you despite your weakness, failure, and sin. However, His using you does not excuse you for your sin, nor does it indicate that God wants you to sin. If you sinned less, God would be able to use you far more powerfully and effectively than is at present possible.

The same is true with healing. *God does not want you to be sick.* Just as He has to accept the fact that you will sin because you misuse the free will He has given you, so He has to accept there may be occasions when you will be sick. This does not mean that He is unable to use you or that He condemns you for being sick. But because sickness is never His will for you, He is always ready to heal and to restore you to His best and finest purpose.

God sent His Son to bring salvation to you.
Jesus wants to forgive you.
Jesus wants to heal you.
Jesus wants to make you whole in spirit, soul, and body.

O LORD, have mercy on me; heal me, for I have sinned against you (Ps. 41:4).

3

THE LORD OUR HEALER

The Trinity of God was involved in creation: Father, Word, and Holy Spirit. By His spoken Word, He created the earth, all the vegetation, and all the living creatures on it. By His spoken Word, He brought man into being: "Then God said, 'Let us make man in our image, in our likeness'" (Gen. 1:26).

THE WORD MADE FLESH

"God saw all that he had made, and it was very good" (Gen. 1:31). The Word through which God created the universe was Jesus. When God spoke, Jesus worked to bring about the creation He desired. Throughout the centuries of the Old Testament, God spoke from heaven. The prophets heard Him speak and interpreted His words to the people. But the time came for the Word of God to become flesh, to take human form, and to live among His people.

John opens his version of the gospel with a great exposition that Jesus is the Word of God: "In the beginning was the Word, and the Word was with God, and the Word was God. He was with God in the beginning. Through him all things were made; without him nothing was made that has been made" (John 1:1–3). When Jesus was born into the world, that Word "became flesh and lived for a while among us" (v. 14). Now all could hear clearly what God wanted to say to His people.

Jesus was involved in the very act of creation. He is the spoken Word of God, so powerful He could bring all creation into being. No wonder then that when Jesus spoke, people were healed. *The Word that created can also heal.*

Even in the days of His humanity, Jesus made it clear that He spoke no words of His own. He spoke only the words that His Father gave Him to speak. When we hear Jesus, we are hearing God the Father speak. "I and the Father are one," Jesus said (John 10:30).

Jesus never acted independently of His Father. He said He could do no works of His own. He did only what pleased His Father, the things He saw His Father doing. *If Jesus healed, it was because He saw His Father healing. He knew that it was the nature of His Father to heal:* "For I have come down from heaven not to do my will but to do the will of him who sent me" (John 6:38).

GOD'S HEALING NATURE

God's nature has not changed. The Bible is an unfolding revelation of who He is. If Jesus healed in His earthly ministry, doing the things He saw His Father doing, that is because healing has always been part of God's nature.

What God created was very good. It was only when first Eve and then Adam succumbed to the temptations of Satan that creation became tainted by sin and evil. The devil had begun his existence as the archangel Lucifer leading the choirs of heaven in worship of the Lord. When he wanted to be like God and to be worshiped himself, he and those who followed him in his rebellion were immediately thrown out of heaven. Jesus said, "I saw Satan fall like lightning from heaven" (Luke 10:18). There could be no room in heaven for any who were evil, rebellious, or disobedient. From that time Satan sought to corrupt creation and to infest it with his evil purposes. The fact that people succumbed to his temptations laid them open to all the other evil he could bring into their lives.

As a result of their sin, Adam and Eve were banished from the garden paradise God created for them. It was not long before Cain murdered his brother Abel. Something worse than sickness was already affecting humankind.

By the time of the Flood, "the earth was corrupt in God's sight and was full of violence. God saw how corrupt the earth had become, for all the people on earth had corrupted their ways" (Gen. 6:11–12). It was hardly surprising therefore that sickness should begin to affect humankind.

Yet God soon revealed that it is His nature to heal His people. After freeing them from Egypt, the land of their captivity, He said to them, "If you listen carefully to the voice of the LORD your God and do what is right in his eyes, if you pay attention to his commands and keep all his decrees, I will not bring on you any of the diseases I brought on the Egyptians, for *I am the LORD, who heals you*" (Exod. 15:26, italics mine). *He heals because it is His nature to heal.*

The implications of what the Lord says are clear: healing is dependent on obedience to His Word and the desire to walk in right ways with Him. Pharaoh's refusal to believe God's words to him and his opposition to God's people had brought about the plagues, diseases, and sicknesses that had afflicted the Egyptians.

Later God reiterates His desire to heal His people: "Worship the LORD your God, and his blessing will be on your food and water. I will take away sickness from among you, and none will miscarry or be barren in your land. I will give you a full life span" (Exod. 23:25–26). God's purpose was to take sickness away from His children and give them a full life span. God's purpose is the same today. He does not desire, in His best and finest purposes, that any of His beloved children should have a premature death.

> *God is still the healer today.*
> *It is His nature to heal.*
> *He wants you to know Him as the Lord who heals you.*

He sent forth his word and healed them (Ps. 107:20).

4

COVENANT FULFILLED

God is faithful. He commits Himself to His people, and He makes them promises that shall never be broken. He entered into a covenant with His people, Israel. A covenant is a binding agreement freely made by two parties. There was no need for God to bind Himself by the terms of any covenant; He chose to do so.

The people were to obey the commandments God gave them, proving themselves faithful to Him. That was their part of the covenant. The Lord, for His part, made solemn promises about the way He would bless His people and cause them to prosper if they were obedient to the commandments.

Throughout the Old Testament, we see God fulfilling His side of the covenant agreement while Israel often failed to honor theirs. Yet He continued to have mercy on His people, lovingly drawing them back to His ways again and again that He might bless them abundantly.

The Lord loves to give to His people; He loves to bless them, to meet their needs and give them the prosperity He desires for them. He wanted the other nations to see how blessed His people were and acknowledge that their God was the only true God.

THE COVENANT NAMES OF GOD

God revealed Himself to Israel under seven covenant names. Each reveals something of God's nature and the way in which He wanted to relate to His people. Because Jesus came to reveal His Father, we see each of these seven names of God being fulfilled in His earthly ministry. Because He is the "Yes" and the "Amen" to all God's promises, Jesus was the means whereby all the promises of the old covenant could be fulfilled in the lives of Christians along with the new promises He gave.

This means that Jesus had to fulfill each of these seven aspects of God's being, not only in His ministry but also on the cross. This fulfillment enabled these blessings to become the inheritance of all who believe in Him. The riches promised through these covenant names, therefore, become the possession of Christians. Each of the covenant names is given in the Old Testament, seen in the ministry of Jesus, fulfilled in the Cross, and seen in the lives of Christians through the working of God's Holy Spirit.

1. *I am with you:*
   • He is the Lord who is present with His people.
   • He was present in a unique way when the Son of God came to live among men and women.
   • Through the Cross, we have been brought near to God

that we might be present with Him eternally: "But now in Christ Jesus you who once were far away have been brought near through the blood of Christ" (Eph. 2:13).

- We are assured of Jesus' presence with us always and of God's presence within us through His gift of the Holy Spirit.

2. *I am your peace:*
   - He is the Lord our peace.
   - Jesus came with the gift of God's peace: "Peace I leave with you; my peace I give you. I do not give to you as the world gives. Do not let your hearts be troubled and do not be afraid" (John 14:27).
   - On the cross, He fulfilled the prophecy: "The punishment that brought us peace was upon him, and by his wounds we are healed" (Isa. 53:5).
   - Now we have peace with God and with others, and His peace is in us as part of the fruit of the Spirit.

3. *I am the Good Shepherd:*
   - He is the Lord our Shepherd. David knew this meant that he would lack nothing.
   - Jesus said, "I am the good shepherd; I know my sheep and my sheep know me" (John 10:14). He came to care for God's children.
   - He said, "I lay down my life for the sheep" (John 10:15).
   - Through the sacrifice of the Shepherd, we have entered His fold, where He loves and cares for us.

4. *I am your provider:*
   - He is the Lord who will provide.
   - Jesus demonstrated His Father's willingness to provide for all His children's needs. He met the needs of all who came to Him: "I have come that they may have life, and have it to the full" (John 10:10).

- The Lord provides a sacrifice for us on the cross that we may belong to Him.
- It is still God's purpose to provide for all our needs, for He gives us everything in Christ: "And my God will meet all your needs according to his glorious riches in Christ Jesus" (Phil. 4:19).

5. *I am your banner:*
   - He is the Lord our banner or victor.
   - Jesus demonstrated His victory over temptation, sin, sickness—the powers of evil in His ministry. He showed that He was ready to fight on behalf of God's children.
   - On the cross, He triumphed over all the powers of Satan: "And having disarmed the powers and authorities, he made a public spectacle of them, triumphing over them by the cross" (Col. 2:15).
   - God has given us the victory through our Lord Jesus Christ.

6. *I am your righteousness:*
   - He is the Lord our righteousness.
   - Jesus came and lived the righteous life here on earth, exposing our unrighteousness.
   - He offered His righteous life to His righteous Father on behalf of our unrighteousness.
   - He has justified us, cleansing us from sins, making us righteous and acceptable in God's sight that we may walk in His ways.

7. *I am your healer:*
   - He is the Lord our healer, the Lord who heals us.
   - Jesus demonstrated His Father's nature and will to heal spiritually, emotionally, and physically.
   - "He took up our infirmities and carried our diseases" to the cross (Matt. 8:17).

• By faith in what He has done, we are able to receive healing of all our diseases.

THE SAME FOREVER

God has not changed throughout the centuries. He is still present with us; He is still our peace. He is our Good Shepherd, our provider, our victor. He is our righteousness, and He is still the Lord our healer.

Why should anyone imagine that He has remained faithful to His covenant nature in all ways except that of healer? Only unbelief leads anyone to such a conclusion.

Why should anyone think that all the aspects of God's covenant nature were fulfilled on the cross—except that of healer? Only spiritual blindness, prejudice, or ignorance of Scripture leads a person to such a conclusion.

Why should anyone believe that only six of the seven are for today? When did God cease to be the Lord who heals? And what possible grounds can there be in Scripture to suggest His healing is not for *all* His children?

No one would question that every other aspect of the Cross is for all. It is only unbelief in His willingness to heal that robs some people of the healing God wants to give them. Do not allow anyone to rob you.

> *Jesus is present with you.*
> *Jesus is your peace.*
> *Jesus is your Shepherd.*
> *Jesus is your provider.*
> *Jesus is your banner.*
> *Jesus is your righteousness.*
> *Jesus is your healer.*

I am the LORD, who heals you (Exod. 15:26).

5

BY HIS STRIPES

Isaiah, chapter 53, gives a remarkable prophecy about the Cross, written hundreds of years before the event, describing how God accomplished our total healing through the crucifixion of Jesus.

When He went to the cross, Jesus not only died for our sins, He carried our sicknesses, infirmities, griefs, and sorrows as well:

> Surely he took up our infirmities
>   and carried our sorrows,
> yet we considered him stricken by God,
>   smitten by him, and afflicted.
> But he was pierced for our transgressions,
>   he was crushed for our iniquities;
> the punishment that brought us peace was upon him,
>   and by his wounds we are healed (vv. 4–5).

Some have interpreted these words to mean only spiritual healing, the restoration of our relationship with God through the forgiveness of sins. That is not a true exposition. The chief way in which we check the meaning and interpretation of any Scripture verse is by other verses. There is absolutely no doubt that the New Testament writers knew these words referred to physical infirmities and sicknesses as well as forgiveness.

Matthew, in chapter 8 of his gospel account, describes several incidents of physical healing from the ministry of Jesus. He writes in verse 16: "When evening came, many who were demon-possessed were brought to him, and he drove out the spirits with a word and healed all the sick." Matthew is definitely writing about demon-possession and physical sickness; Jesus healed all the sick who came to Him regardless of their particular condition. Matthew continues, "This was to fulfill what was spoken through the prophet Isaiah: 'He took up our infirmities and carried our diseases'" (v. 17).

It may seem strange that Matthew says this of Jesus *before* the Crucifixion. But what Jesus did for relatively few during His earthly ministry, He makes possible for all through the Cross. For it was then that His Father caused our sins and sicknesses to be laid on Him. It is possible to translate the Hebrew in verse 10: "Yet it was the Lord's will to crush him and cause him to be sick."

Jesus never sinned, yet He became sin for us. He was never sick, yet He carried our sicknesses on the cross.

What God did for us in Jesus was a total work of healing. The spiritual sickness of our sins was certainly laid upon Him to enable us to receive forgiveness and be reconciled to God, able to enjoy a loving relationship with Him. But He also took our grief, our sorrow, our pains, our diseases, our infirmities—the whole sorry mess. Why? So that we might be set free from these things.

SIN AND SICKNESS CARRIED AWAY

The word translated "carried" means literally that He has lifted them up and carried them away, as one lifts a heavy burden. It is the same word used in reference to what Jesus did for our sins on the cross: "My righteous servant will justify many, and he will bear their iniquities" (Isa. 53:11); "For he bore the sin of many, and made intercession for the transgressors" (v. 12).

On the cross, Jesus dealt with sicknesses and pains in the same way that He dealt with sin: He carried them away. He took them upon Himself that we might be freed from them all. Of course He dealt with grief and sorrow also, for "he was oppressed and afflicted" (Isa. 53:7), suffering mental and emotional turmoil that we might be set free from such problems.

JESUS' HEALING SACRIFICE FOR ALL

Faith for healing is not attempting to believe that God *will* do something; it is trusting in what He has already done and made available through the Cross. It is inconsistent to say that Jesus died for your sins without also saying that He died for your sicknesses.

It is equally inconsistent to claim that the forgiveness available because of Jesus' atoning work on the cross is for all but His healing work is only for some.

It is also inconsistent to say that Jesus died to forgive sins in every generation but to heal only in the apostolic age. His atoning work is for all people at all times and covers God's healing purposes for us completely—spirit, soul, and body.

Jesus died for us *all* and included every need in what He did. He took up *our* infirmities. He carried *our* sorrows. He was pierced for *our* transgressions. He was crushed for *our* iniquities. The punishment that brought *us* peace was upon Him, and by His wounds *we* are healed.

If we were taught from the beginning of our Christian lives that it is just as natural to come to the cross and say, "Lord, by what You did for me there, heal me," as it is to come to Him and say, "Lord, through what You did for me on the cross, forgive me," we would see much more healing among Christians today.

Most of us have faith to believe that God forgives our sins because that teaching has been instilled in us throughout our Christian lives; but many are actually taught the opposite when it comes to other aspects of God's healing. Do not rely on the opinions of people or their interpretations; *go by what the Word of God actually says.* The Word will often challenge your thinking and your experience, but these are words of truth. *By the stripes of Jesus you are healed—totally.*

You are included in all Jesus did on the cross. Through His sacrifice, you can receive forgiveness of sins and healing of every disease.

By sending Jesus to die for you, God has demonstrated He wants to forgive you and to heal you.

Jesus has already done everything that needs to be done to make your healing possible.

Jesus wants you to have faith in what He has done.

He took up our infirmities and carried our diseases (Matt. 8:17).

6

THE PROPHECY FULFILLED

Have you ever wondered why the gospel accounts give so much detail to the events of the passion? One quarter of

Mark's gospel, for example, is given over to these events, which took place within a few hours. The evangelists had to be very selective in their use of material, so they would not have recorded the Cross in such detail unless there were important reasons for doing so.

The details are significant because they describe how Jesus fulfilled completely the prophecy of Isaiah 53.

JESUS TAKES OUR NEEDS

From the moment Judas leaves the Last Supper, a significant change takes place in Jesus' ministry. Until that moment He has ministered to people, meeting their needs, healing the sick, and delivering them from demonic bondage. Now, instead of meeting needs, He takes the needs upon Himself, allowing things to happen to Him; He *suffers* these things. The only exception occurs at the time of His arrest in the garden when He heals the high priest's servant after Peter has cut off his ear. He rectifies His disciple's mistake.

When Judas leaves the Last Supper to betray Jesus, He suffers that betrayal; He carries the burden of it; He allows it to happen to Him. This would have been uncharacteristic of His earlier ministry when Jesus was in control of every situation. He lets the enemy have his way; He carries the betrayal of one of His friends.

Within the next few hours, Peter denies Jesus three times, despite his affirmation that he will never do such a thing. When Jesus turns and looks at him, Peter weeps, full of remorse. Jesus suffers that denial; He takes it upon Himself.

As He kneels in prayer in the Garden of Gethsemane, He experiences intense mental anguish and anxiety. *He is taking on Himself all the mental conflict we can ever experience.* He suffers such mental torment to free us from anguish and anxiety.

At His hour of greatest need, all His disciples desert Him, leaving Him to suffer alone: Jesus suffers that rejection by His closest friends.

When arrested, He is taken before the high priests, Annas and Caiaphas, and Pilate, the Roman governor. When falsely accused, He does not try to defend Himself. He suffers all the false accusations and lies. Only when directly challenged as to His true identity does He speak. To remain silent would have been a denial of the truth.

We feel indignant when unjustly accused. Jesus suffered a greater injustice. He carried to the cross all our injustices— even persecution for the sake of the gospel of truth.

The crowd calls for His blood, demanding that He suffer the cruel death by crucifixion. These same people whom Jesus had loved, taught, and healed turn on Him now. As if the rejection of His friends was not enough, He has to carry the rejection of the world.

He allows Himself to be condemned, taking all condemnation upon Himself, making it possible for those who believe in Him to be freed from all condemnation. We deserve to be condemned because we sin against God; we deserve death. But Jesus suffered the penalty we deserve; He bore our punishment for us, receiving the death sentence that would free us from death.

He is mocked and beaten by the soldiers, taking the ridicule that is heaped on Him. Why did the Father let all these things happen to His beloved Son? Why should such details be recorded for us in the Gospels? Would it not have been enough to say that Jesus was crucified and took our sins upon Himself? No, these things are recorded because they are all-important.

EVEN PHYSICAL PAIN

When Jesus stood bearing the lashes from the Roman soldiers, all our physical pain and sicknesses were being heaped upon Him. He never sinned; He was never sick; but He took upon Himself our sins and all our pains and sicknesses. It is as if one lash was for cancer, another for bone disease, another for heart disease, and so on. *Everything that causes physical pain was laid on Jesus as the nails were driven into His hands and feet. By the wounds of Jesus we are healed.*

It was not the lashes that produced healing but the fact that our heavenly Father was laying all our sicknesses on His Son, so immense is His love for us. He allowed Jesus to suffer in that way to set us free from all that was laid on Him.

No wonder when Jesus was led to Calvary He was unable to carry His cross up the hill. The fact that the wooden cross was laid on another is significant. Jesus was climbing that hill with a burden of much greater importance than a piece of wood. *He was carrying betrayal, failure, mental anguish, rejection, injustice, ridicule, condemnation, and all the sins of humankind. He was taking all the grief and sorrow, all the pains and sicknesses of God's people so that they might be set free from them all.* Let another carry the wood; Jesus was carrying you and me.

REJECTED

What a sorry tale of rejection! Rejected by Judas, by Peter, by all the twelve disciples; rejected by Annas and Caiaphas, by Pilate, by the crowd, by the soldiers, and by those who mocked Him at the foot of the cross. He took all that rejection upon Himself.

Jesus is the One through whom you can be healed of every

sense of rejection, inadequacy, and inferiority—He takes it all. No wonder He cried out on the cross, "My God, my God, why have you forsaken me?" (Matt. 27:46).

These are mighty words because when He uttered them, Jesus demonstrated that He identified completely with us in our condition. He experienced what we have known well, separation from God the Father. Although He never sinned, He experienced this separation to bring us back to fellowship with God.

But it was not long afterward that Jesus said, "Father, into your hands I commit my spirit" (Luke 23:46). He died in victory, not in defeat; He was taking all who believed in Him to the Father.

He was raised from the dead in victory. That resurrection demonstrates that He overcame death, sin, and all the works of Satan, including sickness and disease. By the stripes of Jesus we *are* healed.

He became a curse to free you from everything that can be a curse in your life, even the curse of formalized, legalistic religion, which denies the power of God today: "Christ redeemed us from the curse of the law by becoming a curse for us, for it is written: 'Cursed is everyone who is hung on a tree'" (Gal. 3:13). He wants you to have a living faith in Him and in all He has done for you on the cross.

> *By the wounds of Jesus you have been healed.*
> *He took every need you could ever have upon Himself to free you from your need.*
> *He was stripped of everything, taking even poverty to the cross.*

The punishment that brought us peace was upon him, and by his wounds we are healed (Isa. 53:5).

||||||||||||||||||||||||||||||||||||||||||||||

Part Two

FAITH FOR YOUR
HEALING

||||||||||||||||||||||||||||||||||||||||||||||

7

FACTS AND FAITH

God taught Abraham the principles of living by faith, stepping out in obedience to His word. He told him to leave his country and go to the land He would show him: "So Abram left, as the LORD had told him" (Gen. 12:4). When God speaks, He expects obedience, the obedience of faith. *Faith is not simply believing that God has spoken; it is acting upon what He has said.*

When Sarah laughed at God's promise that she would have a child although she was barren and past the age of childbearing, God said to Abraham, "Is anything too hard for the LORD? I will return to you at the appointed time next year and Sarah will have a son" (Gen. 18:14). If God speaks, His purpose will surely be performed. Even the physical restriction of old age was not enough to prevent God from giving Abraham and Sarah the son for whom they longed.

We are used to dealing with physical facts, yet what God says challenges the facts as we perceive them. Abraham was nearly a hundred years old and Sarah was long past the age for childbearing when God said they would have a son. Little wonder the idea seemed laughable. Yet, "by faith Abraham, even though he was past age—and Sarah herself was barren— was enabled to become a father because he considered him faithful who had made the promise" (Heb. 11:11).

So Isaac was born and Abraham became the father of a multitude of nations, as God had promised.

The facts said that Abraham and Sarah could have no children. God said they would have a son—and He never lies. *He is faithful and watches over His Word to perform it.*

Facts are facts, but they are not the ultimate truth for believers. Your faith needs to be based on God's Word, not on the facts. That does not mean that you deny the existence of the facts; that means you recognize that *God has the power to change the facts.*

GOD'S WORD CHALLENGES THE FACTS

Moses and the Israelites were trapped between the Red Sea and the Egyptian army that pursued them. That was a fact. Their situation seemed hopeless because they had no means of defending themselves against the might of their pursuers. But God told Moses to stretch out his hand, and when Moses obeyed, God parted the Red Sea and His people crossed over on dry land. When the Egyptians followed, the waters came together again, and they drowned.

The word God spoke to Moses challenged the facts, and when he acted on that word, the facts changed.

Sometimes the words the Lord spoke to His servants seemed almost absurd. How could the walls of a city fall down simply because His people marched around them for seven days and seven times on the seventh day? The walls fell because the people believed the word God spoke to them and acted on it! "When the trumpets sounded, the people shouted, and at the sound of the trumpet, when the people gave a loud shout, the wall collapsed; so every man charged straight in, and they took the city" (Josh. 6:20). They followed precisely the instructions given them by the Lord.

This is not to say that people *want* to obey the Lord's word to them. Elisha told Naaman through a messenger to wash seven times in the River Jordan to be healed of his leprosy. Naaman, a mighty general, was deeply offended:

"I thought that he [Elisha] would surely come out to me and stand and call on the name of the LORD his God, wave his hand over the spot and cure me of my leprosy. Are not Abana and Pharpar, the rivers of Damascus, better than any of the waters of Israel? Couldn't I wash in them and be cleansed?" So he turned and went off in a rage (2 Kings 5:11–12).

Naaman's servants pointed out to him that he would have been happy to do some great deed if asked, so why should he object to such a simple request? Naaman then humbled himself before his own men, and "he went down and dipped himself in the Jordan seven times, as the man of God had told him, and his flesh was restored and became clean like that of a young boy" (v. 14).

No doubt the tension was great after the sixth submersion. But God was faithful to His word—as He always is. Once again we see that His word has the power to change the facts, even the fact of physical disease.

JESUS CHALLENGES THE FACTS

Jesus taught His disciples the same lesson. If they put their faith in the facts, they would miss God's purpose. If they believed His words, they would see His supernatural power at work, changing the facts.

Take, for example, the feeding of the five thousand. Jesus did not want to send the people away hungry, and He suggested that His disciples feed them. Their response was rational; they looked at the facts and raised two reasonable objections.

First, they asked where they could buy bread in such a remote place. Their second objection was that they had insufficient money to buy bread for such a crowd: "Eight months' wages would not buy enough bread for each one to have a bite!" (John 6:7).

This rational approach omits the possibility of God's supernatural power. Jesus approached every situation knowing that the resources of God's heavenly kingdom were available to Him. He put His faith not in the facts but in the truth that could change the facts.

When He took what was available—five loaves and two small fish—and blessed them, the disciples were able to feed all the people and collect twelve baskets full of the remains. That abundance demonstrates the power of faith over the facts.

Every time a person came to Him for healing, Jesus trusted what His Father was able to do to change the facts. He was well aware of the existence of the facts; He did not deny that facts are facts. But He chose to put His faith in His Father, not in the facts.

When you are faced with a serious problem, the situation may seem hopeless, but there is great hope in the power of God.

> *For God, nothing is impossible.*
> *His word to you can change the facts.*
> *Don't believe the facts and miss His purpose; believe what*
>   *He is able to do to change the facts.*
> Jesus is the Lord your healer.

So is my word that goes out from my mouth:
    It will not return to me empty,
but will accomplish what I desire
    and achieve the purpose for which I sent it (Isa. 55:11).

8

JESUS WANTS TO HEAL

Jesus is the Word of God who became flesh and dwelt among men and women, bringing them the good news of His kingdom. As God created by His Word, so He healed through that Word, Jesus.

It is obvious from the gospel accounts that healing occupied a great deal of Jesus' time and attention during His ministry. He preached day after day to great multitudes, not only speaking about the kingdom of God but demonstrating its presence and power. He used the authority of the kingdom to bring healing into the lives of His people.

EVERY DISEASE HEALED

Several statements testify to the fact that He healed every kind of sickness and disease. For example: "Jesus went throughout Galilee, teaching in their synagogues, preaching the good news of the kingdom, and healing every disease and sickness among the people" (Matt. 4:23). He healed all who came to Him to be healed: "News about him spread all over Syria, and people brought to him all who were ill with various diseases, those suffering severe pain, the demon-possessed, those having seizures, and the paralyzed, and he healed them" (v. 24).

In the midst of a great multitude of people God never loses sight of the individual. In the gospel accounts we have not only these general statements about Jesus healing but also the record of how He ministered to specific individuals in need.

JESUS FULFILLS PROPHECIES

At the beginning of His ministry, Jesus went to the synagogue in His hometown of Nazareth and read from the prophecy of Isaiah:

> The Spirit of the Sovereign LORD is on me,
> because the LORD has anointed me
> to preach the good news to the poor.
> He has sent me to bind up the brokenhearted,
> to proclaim freedom for the captives
> and release from darkness for the prisoners,
> to proclaim the year of the LORD's favor
> and the day of vengeance of our God,
> to comfort all who mourn,
> and provide for those who grieve in Zion—
> to bestow on them a crown of beauty
> instead of ashes,
> the oil of gladness
> instead of mourning,
> and a garment of praise
> instead of a spirit of despair (Isa. 61:1–3).

The Father sent His Son to undo all the negative things that can happen in the lives of His people. "Today this scripture is fulfilled in your hearing," Jesus said (Luke 4:21). He came to bring spiritual liberty but also to deal with the brokenhearted, with everything that causes people to grieve and mourn.

Jesus came to fulfill other prophetic words spoken about His ministry:

> Then will the eyes of the blind be opened
> and the ears of the deaf unstopped.
> Then will the lame leap like a deer,
> and the mute tongue shout for joy (Isa. 35:5–6).

Through Him, spiritually blind and deaf people would come to see and hear the truth. Because He came with the power of God's kingdom, physically blind people would have their eyes opened and physically deaf people would be able to hear, people with mobility impairments would be healed and people without speech would sing God's praises.

The Sermon on the Mount is followed immediately by Jesus' demonstration of the gospel in action. Paul said several years later, "For the kingdom of God is not a matter of talk but of power" (1 Cor. 4:20). Jesus taught the gospel of the kingdom, and the works of the kingdom that He performed verified His message. The signs and wonders God did through Him confirmed His words. As Nicodemus, one of the Pharisees, remarked, "Rabbi, we know you are a teacher who has come from God. For no one could perform the miraculous signs you are doing if God were not with him" (John 3:2).

JESUS WANTS TO HEAL

The first person to come to Jesus for healing was a man with leprosy who said, "Lord, if you are willing, you can make me clean" (Matt. 8:2).

Many people today approach the Lord with a similar tentativeness. They know God is able to heal, and perhaps they believe He wants to heal; but in their hearts they question, Is He going to heal me of this particular condition?

The man with leprosy came to Jesus with this conditional *if*. Jesus simply removed the *if* and answered, "I am willing. . . . Be clean!" (Matt. 8:3). And immediately, the man was cured of his leprosy.

It is always God's best purpose to heal. When you come tentatively with an *if*, the first thing He wants to do is to remove the *if* from your thinking.

Having declared that He wanted to heal the man, Jesus did not pray long prayers over him; He spoke the word of healing, and immediately, the leprosy was healed.

Does this incident demonstrate only that it was the Lord's purpose to heal that particular man at that particular moment? No, its significance is much greater. Jesus said He could do nothing by Himself; He did only what He saw His Father doing. He had come not to do His own will but to do that of His Father who sent Him. Jesus would not heal unless He saw His Father healing, unless He knew that to be His Father's will and purpose. *Because it was His Father's nature to heal, He could be sure of what He wanted to do for the man with leprosy, and for all who came to Him for healing. Because His Father always wants to heal, Jesus wanted to heal.* He spoke the words, *I am willing* on behalf of His Father and Himself.

Jesus did not have long prayer sessions with His Father inquiring whether He wanted to heal; He knew what His Father wanted to do. Every time we see Jesus performing a miracle or healing a sick person, we see His Father working in and through Him. When He speaks words of healing, He speaks the words His Father gives Him to speak, for He said, "I speak no words of My own. I speak only the words My Father gives Me to speak." (See John 8:28–29.)

In this, as in every other incident in His life, Jesus is doing what He knows His Father would do. The Father speaks through His Son, works through His Son, and is glorified in the events of His Son's life. Jesus would not do anything unless it was completely and wholeheartedly God's will.

Do you feel tentative in your approach to Jesus? Understand the following points:

> *It is Jesus' purpose to heal you and meet your need.*
> *It is His nature to heal, and His desire is to give to you.*
> *Let Jesus take away all your ifs and buts.*
> *Hear His word to you now.*

I am willing. . . . Be clean! (Matt. 8:3).

9

ONE WORD FROM GOD

A Roman centurion came to Jesus and said, "Lord, . . . my servant lies at home paralyzed and in terrible suffering" (Matt. 8:6). The act of faith is for people to come to Jesus. There are very few occasions when He initiates the healing; for the most part He responds to the faith of those who come to Him. He did not heal every sick person in Israel, but Scripture affirms that He did heal *all who came to Him.*

COMING TO JESUS WITH FAITH

The man with leprosy came tentatively; the centurion came with a quality of faith that astonished Jesus. He knew he was unworthy to have Jesus in his house and considered this unnecessary when Jesus offered to come and heal the servant. The centurion said, "But just say the word, and my servant will be healed" (v. 8). How could this man exhibit such faith? Because he understood the power of authority and recognized Jesus to be a man of authority.

The centurion knew what it was to be under authority; he had to obey his superiors. He knew also how to exercise authority over those under him. As soon as he gave an order, he expected instant obedience. *Because he recognized the authority Jesus possessed, he believed Jesus could command the sickness to leave his servant. Jesus only had to give the order.*

This is the quality of faith God desires to see in all His children. They recognize the supreme lordship and authority of Jesus. He has power over all things, including every sickness and disease you could ever experience. *One word from Him is enough to effect your healing.*

Jesus said to those following Him: "I tell you the truth, I have not found anyone in Israel with such great faith" (v. 10). That included His own disciples! Nobody else had shown such faith in Jesus because nobody else had recognized His authority in that way.

THE AUTHORITY OF JESUS

Even Jesus' opponents came to understand He was the man of authority. "By what authority are you doing these things?" they asked. "Who gave you this authority?" (Matt. 21:23). Demons responded immediately when addressed by Jesus; sickness left people's bodies; even the wind and waves obeyed Him. How much more should those who profess to have faith in Him respect the power and authority of His Word.

He only had to speak, and healing was performed. There was no need for Jesus to make a journey to the centurion's house. He only had to say, "It is done," and it was done. Faith is believing His words have such power and authority.

Because the centurion believed, Jesus acted accordingly,

for He always responds to the precise nature of the faith expressed in Him: "'Go! It will be done just as you believed it would.' And his servant was healed at that very hour" (Matt. 8:13).

A nurse was critically ill some years ago. She was on a life-support system and unable to communicate with anyone. The medical staff were unaware that she could understand what they were saying about the hopelessness of her case.

She could not speak, but she could hear—not only those around her but the Lord as well. She heard His Word being spoken to her heart, "by his wounds you have been healed" (1 Pet. 2:24). To Him, her case was not hopeless.

At first those words seemed to be held out to her as a lifeline. Then she came to realize that her healing had taken place when Jesus died on the cross. She made a remarkable recovery to the amazement of her doctors.

Jesus wants to speak words of faith to your heart by the Holy Spirit. Faith comes from hearing His Word spoken to you personally. When you receive His Word with faith, you recognize His authority over the circumstances that concern you. Unbelief calls God a liar and says His words are not true. Unbelief questions the authority of Jesus and His power to meet a particular need.

You believe in Jesus.
His words are truth to your heart.
As you read the Scriptures, pray that the Holy Spirit will make Jesus' words personal to you.
His words are spirit and life; they are healing to your whole body.
Your situation is not impossible: one word from Jesus can change everything.

Go! It will be done just as you believed it would (Matt. 8:13).

10

THE STRETCHER OF FAITH

A paralyzed man was brought to Jesus on a stretcher of faith. The stretcher was real enough, but it was faith that brought the man to the healer and faith that caused his friends to let him down through the roof so that Jesus could minister to him.

Jesus *saw* their faith. Faith says, "If I come to Jesus, He will heal me because He has already carried all my sins, sorrows, and sicknesses to the cross." In essence faith is utterly simple. It is trusting God, trusting in what He has done and said. Faith is never based on feelings; it is based on God's Word brought to our hearts by the Holy Spirit.

Only when people were demon-possessed did Jesus not expect to see faith. He knew the demon activity within such people would lead them away from Him, not toward Him in faith.

THE HEART OF THE NEED

The men who brought their paralyzed friend had a simple faith. They trusted that Jesus could heal their friend. His problems were spiritual as well as physical, and Jesus always went straight to the heart of the need. He looks not at the symptoms but at what lies beneath them. He is concerned not only with the cause of the sickness but also with anything that could hinder the receiving of healing, whether it seems directly related to the specific need or not.

Jesus perceived that the man needed forgiveness. That is true of everybody who comes to the Lord for healing. In this case I believe that Jesus perceived that the paralysis from which the man was suffering was the direct cause of guilt.

Even if not the cause, guilt was certainly hindering him from receiving the healing Jesus wanted to give him. That is the destructive nature of guilt. Above all else the man needed to hear that his sins were forgiven. Jesus did not pray a long prayer over the man but told him, "Your sins are forgiven" (Matt. 9:2).

Whenever we come to the Lord for healing, this assurance is the first thing we need to hear in our hearts from God: *Your sins are forgiven.* Then we can have confidence not only that God wants to give us the healing we need but also that there is nothing to hinder us from receiving that healing.

AUTHORITY TO FORGIVE—AND HEAL

The Pharisees and others standing around thought it blasphemous that Jesus should dare to pronounce forgiveness of sins. He knew their thoughts and asked them, "Which is easier: to say, 'Your sins are forgiven,' or to say, 'Get up and walk'?" Then He turned to the paralyzed man and said, "Get up, take your mat and go home." And the paralyzed man got up, completely healed. Again it was by speaking a word of authority that Jesus healed. The man responded to the word; he didn't lie there saying, "I can't. I'm paralyzed." *He responded with faith and acted on the word of Jesus and was healed.*

Jesus made it perfectly clear to the spectators why He was doing what He did. They questioned His authority to forgive sins. As many have pointed out over the centuries, forgiveness is the greatest healing miracle of all, that God should wash away all our guilt and make us spotless in His sight. Jesus was prepared to give definite and visible evidence that He had authority to forgive. He told the man to get up and walk "so that you may know that the Son of Man has authority on earth to forgive sins" (v. 6).

Jesus' words provide a great challenge to the church today. Should not those who proclaim the gospel of the forgiveness of sins verify the authenticity of their words by healing the sick? Does God not promise to confirm His words with signs following? Neither Jesus nor the apostolic church expected people to believe a gospel of words only. They demonstrated the truth of those words with the power of God. *Our authority to heal verifies our authority to assure people of their forgiveness.* One substantiates the other. Do we really fulfill the commission of Jesus if we only say to people, "Your sins are forgiven you," without verifying that we have such authority by also saying, "Get up and walk"? Backing up words with authority and power is a challenge to the faith of every believer.

FORGIVE AND BE FORGIVEN

The Lord wants to do a total work of healing in your life. Are you burdened by a sense of guilt or aware of sin that needs His forgiveness? Is so, confess your sins to Him now. Don't delay. Know He will honor His Word: "If we claim to be without sin, we deceive ourselves and the truth is not in us. If we confess our sins, he is faithful and just and will forgive us our sins and purify us from all unrighteousness" (1 John 1:8–9).

Forgive any who have wronged you, for Jesus teaches us, "For if you forgive men when they sin against you, your heavenly Father will also forgive you. But if you do not forgive men their sins, your Father will not forgive your sins" (Matt. 6:14–15). This teaching demonstrates how important it is to forgive those who have hurt you or wronged you in any way. Don't hold on to bitterness, anger, or resentment. Such things are like spiritual cancer eating away at your life, and they can lead to physical sickness as well as emotional pain.

Don't let the devil deceive you. He often tries to suggest to Christians that they do not mean what they say, that their forgiveness of others is not real. Forgiveness is not a feeling; it is an act of the will. It will help you to say aloud, "Lord Jesus, I forgive..." Do not go over all the details of the offense; that is not necessary. Just forgive those responsible and then pray for them that they, too, may know the love and peace of Jesus. Even if those concerned have since died, you still need to forgive them for your own sake.

As you forgive others, the forgiveness and healing of Jesus come into your life. As He forgives you for your sins, the way is open for you to receive the healing you need.

---

*Hear the Master say to you, "Your sins are forgiven."
They are gone—forever.
God will never hold those things against you or even
remember them.
When God forgives, He forgets.
It is as if those things never happened.
Jesus, who died for your sins, carried your sicknesses to
the cross.
Jesus wants you to receive your healing.*

Take heart, son; your sins are forgiven (Matt. 9:2).

11

TOUCH AND BE TOUCHED

The ruler of a synagogue came to Jesus and said, "My daughter has just died. But come and put your hand on her, and she will live" (Matt. 9:18). Again someone came to Jesus with faith, but it was of a different kind from that of either the man with leprosy or the centurion. The man with leprosy came with tentative faith: "If you are willing, you can make me clean" (8:2). The centurion said, "But just say the word, and my servant will be healed" (8:8). This man said, "But come and put your hand on her, and she will live." Jesus went with him.

COME AND TOUCH

Jesus always responds to the precise nature of the faith with which He is given to work. The centurion said, "Just say the word, and my servant will be healed"; so Jesus spoke and the servant was healed at that very hour. The ruler said, "Come and put your hand on her, and she will live"; then Jesus responded to his faith and went with the man to his house.

A large crowd followed Him as He went. It is not difficult to imagine people flocking to Him not only because they wanted to hear His teaching but also because they knew that He was a man who met needs.

IF I TOUCH

One of the women in this crowd had faith of yet a different quality: "She said to herself, 'If I only touch his cloak, I will be healed'" (9:21). Mark's gospel reports that she "had been subject to bleeding for twelve years. She had suffered a great deal under the care of many doctors and had spent all she had, yet instead of getting better she grew worse" (5:25–26). She had tried natural means of healing, and none of them had worked. She needed God to do something supernatural; she needed a miracle. She was obviously a fearful, self-conscious person, like many of us, and didn't want to make herself conspicuous. Yet in her desperation to be healed after so many years of sickness, she was determined to touch Jesus. As she did so, her bleeding stopped, and she felt in her body that she was freed. At the same time Jesus knew power had gone out of Him, for He had been touched not only by a woman's hand but by *faith*. "Who touched my clothes?" He asked. The disciples were utterly perplexed. Fancy asking such a question with so many people thronging around! "But Jesus kept looking around to see who had done it" (Mark 5:30–32).

We can imagine this dear woman cringing with fear. She falls trembling at His feet. Her fear is unfounded: Jesus only wants to commend her. "Daughter, your faith has healed you. Go in peace and be freed from your suffering," He says (v. 34).

Again Jesus emphasizes the importance of faith when needing to receive healing from Him. We certainly see the centrality of faith in what Jesus teaches about prayer and healing, by both His words and His actions. *Your faith has healed you.* This does not mean that faith itself does the healing; faith in Jesus enables God to release His healing power.

The woman who came and touched Jesus' garment was saying to herself, "If I just touch Him, I have it"; that's faith. The centurion said, "You speak, Jesus, and my servant has it"; that's faith, appropriating what God makes available. They were not being vague, saying that God would give them their healing in some way at some time in the future. Faith says, "I have it!"

Was that woman the only one who touched Jesus and was healed? No. "They begged him to let them touch even the edge of his cloak, and *all who touched him were healed*" (Mark 6:56, italics mine)—not all those who jostled Him in the crowd but all who touched Him with faith.

PRAY WITH FAITH

We cannot touch Jesus physically, but we are able to touch Him with our prayers of faith. Sometimes prayer leads to a sudden and dramatic healing. At other times symptoms may persist for a time, but as we continue to stand in faith, the healing is completed. Such a period can be a real testing of faith! But we are able to come through that because we have received revelation; we know in our hearts that we have received the answer. If we receive the truth in our spirits, our minds, emotions, and physical beings respond to that truth.

Nowhere does Jesus teach us to pray with vague hope that something might happen in the future; He teaches us to believe we have received the answer: "Therefore I tell you, whatever you ask for in prayer, believe that you have received it, and it will be yours" (Mark 11:24).

Vague prayers receive vague answers; specific prayers receive specific answers.

The ruler said to Jesus, "Come and put your hand on her, and she will live." That is not a vague hope that something might happen at some time in the future. He believed Jesus would restore his daughter to life as soon as He touched her—that's faith! He believed the answer to her need.

DON'T BE AFRAID; JUST BELIEVE

When Jesus came to the house, He first cleared out all the noisy people who were wailing and lamenting over the girl's death. At the same time He spoke His own faith: "The girl is not dead but asleep" (Matt. 9:24). They laughed at Him, for they knew she was physically dead. They believed the facts—not what God was able to do to change the facts.

Jesus wanted to get all the unbelief out of the way. He told the ruler, "Don't be afraid; just believe" (Mark 5:36). Again that emphasis on faith! He took the girl by the hand and said to her, "Little girl, I say to you, get up!" (v. 41). Immediately, she stood up and walked around.

It seems so simple. Those at the house were full of unbelief, but Jesus responded to her father's faith: "Jesus, come. Touch her. She *will* be healed." Jesus came, He touched her, and she *was* healed. There was no *if* or *but* or *maybe* as far as the father was concerned. He was expressing faith—not hope!

Sometimes we pray long prayers trying to convince God we really believe He is able to do what we need. Actually, there is a great simplicity about faith, and God knows when we truly believe in our hearts.

What can you do if you sense that you do not have faith to meet the need? How can you obtain that faith?

Jesus is the author and perfecter of your faith. He gives faith as a gift of the Holy Spirit. Faith comes from hearing His Word in your heart. If you need faith you do not have, come to Jesus and first confess the sin of your unbelief. Let Him forgive you and clear that out of the way. Then ask for the gift of faith from the Holy Spirit.

Now turn to the Scriptures and ask the Holy Spirit to witness to you the truth of God's healing words.

> *I am the LORD, who heals you (Exod. 15:26).*
> *[He] forgives all your sins and heals all your diseases (Ps. 103:3).*
> *Surely he took up our infirmities and carried our sorrows . . . and by his wounds we are healed (Isa. 53:4–5).*
> *My words . . . are life to those who find them and health to a man's whole body (Prov. 4:20, 22).*
> *You restored me to health and let me live (Isa. 38:16).*
> *I am willing. . . . Be clean! (Matt. 8:3).*
> *Go! It will be done just as you believed it would (Matt. 8:13).*

Don't be afraid; just believe (Mark 5:36).

12

A MATTER OF GRACE

Bartimaeus was a blind beggar. While sitting by the road begging, he heard the noise of the crowd surrounding Jesus coming in his direction. No doubt he had heard about the wonderful healings that were taking place as Jesus ministered to people. It was too good an opportunity to be missed.

He began to shout, "Jesus, Son of David, have mercy on me!" (Mark 10:47). Others around him rebuked him, telling him to be quiet. Perhaps they thought that Jesus would not be interested in someone rejected by society. Perhaps they were offended by his assertion that Jesus was the Son of David, a clear affirmation that He was the Messiah.

Bartimaeus took no notice of them. His need far outweighed their opinions. He shouted with even greater determination, "Son of David, have mercy on me!" (v. 48).

Jesus must have heard his cry for mercy, for He said to those around him, "Call him" (v. 49). The attitude of the crowd changed immediately. Instead of trying to silence the beggar, they said to him, "Cheer up! On your feet! He's calling you" (v. 49).

We can imagine his eagerness as he groped his way toward Jesus.

A SIMPLE QUESTION

"What do you want me to do for you?" Jesus asked him (Mark 10:51). That question may seem strange, for Bartimaeus's need must have been obvious. But Jesus had the habit of asking simple, direct questions to draw out faith from those who came to Him. He knew how important it was for that faith to be expressed on their lips.

The question is not quite as obvious as it seems at first. It should never be taken for granted that someone coming for prayer actually wants to be healed. For some people, sickness has become part of their identity, and they are afraid to be healed lest in some way they lose their identity. They fear that others will relate to them differently and that they will not receive the sympathy and attention given them before.

Bartimaeus's answer is straightforward: "Rabbi, I want to

see." He makes a simple statement of faith, for he plainly believes that Jesus is able *and willing* to give him his sight back. Jesus rewards his faith: "*'Go . . . your faith has healed you.'* Immediately he received his sight and followed Jesus along the road" (v. 52, italics mine).

Again Scripture emphasizes faith as the basis of the healing! Again Jesus speaks only a word of authority, and the blindness is healed.

The way Bartimaeus approached Jesus is important, for he came not only having faith but knowing he needed to receive mercy from Jesus.

THE GOD OF GRACE

No one ever deserves to receive healing from the Lord. It makes no difference how good a Christian she is, how greatly she has been used of God, nobody deserves of herself to receive anything from the Lord. However, our God is the Lord of grace. He gives His gifts to those who deserve nothing. He deals with us not as we deserve but through His love, graciousness, and generosity.

Whenever you come to God in prayer, He is ready to have mercy on you, to forgive you as you confess your sins to Him, and to give to you out of His abundant mercy and grace: "And God is able to make all grace abound to you, so that in all things at all times, having all that you need, you will abound in every good work" (2 Cor. 9:8).

That is the measure of grace God shows to *you*. He desires to show you His generosity in such a way that in *all* things at *all* times, you may have *all* that you need. *All* means *all*. Don't change God's Word because of any unbelief.

He wants to answer all your prayers, not some of them.

He is interested in every situation in your life, not just a few of them.

He wants to meet all your needs, not only those that are so big you feel you cannot cope with them.

The immensity of God's grace challenges us. John tells us that Jesus "came from the Father, full of grace and truth" (John 1:14).

There is never a moment of any day or night when God does not want to give to you. As a Christian, you are a child of God's grace: "From the fullness of his grace we have all received one blessing after another" (v. 16).

Notice the word *all* again; we have *all* received. To whom does this refer? "Yet to all who received him, to those who believed in his name, he gave the right to become children of God" (v. 12). *If you have put your faith in Jesus and received Him as your Lord, you are a child of God, a child of grace; and Jesus wants you to receive one blessing after another from the fullness of His grace.*

Don't be put off from coming to Jesus with your need by any sense of unworthiness. Don't hide behind pseudo-spiritual statements that are only a cover for unbelief: "There are many others far worse off than I am." "I don't want to trouble the Lord with my problems." "I don't want to take up His time."

God's grace and power are so immense that He is able to meet every need in every person who calls on Him. He is not like a man, able to concentrate on only one thing at a time.

Approach the Lord not tentatively but with positive determination like Bartimaeus.

Jesus is willing to have mercy on you.

Jesus is willing to heal you.

Jesus wants to say to you, "Go, your faith has healed you."

And God is able to make all grace abound to you, so that in all things at all times, having all that you need, you will abound in every good work (2 Cor. 9:8).

13

COMPASSION ON ALL

One of the very few occasions when Jesus initiated a healing concerned the man who had been "an invalid for thirty-eight years." He was one of a great number of blind people and people with other impairments who used to lie around the Pool of Bethesda. It was common belief that the water had healing properties when "stirred."

Why Jesus should have picked him out of that mass of human need is not clear, but when He learned he had been an invalid for so long, He asked him, "Do you want to get well?" (John 5:6). Jesus did not take it for granted that the man wanted to be healed.

His reply indicated his genuine desire to be healed, and so Jesus spoke the word of authority to him. No mention of faith here; Jesus simply manifested God's graciousness. He promises to give us what we believe; because He is gracious, He sometimes heals when there is a lack of faith on the part of the sick person.

EVANGELISTIC HEALING

Healing apart from faith is particularly the case in evangelistic situations. When Jesus sent the seventy-two disciples, He told them, "When you enter a town and are welcomed, eat what is set before you. Heal the sick who are there and tell them, 'The kingdom of God is near you'" (Luke 10:8–9).

Here the order seems to be accept the hospitality you are offered, heal those who are sick, and then tell them why they have been healed—because you have brought them the good news of the kingdom of God.

Jesus doesn't ask for faith from those who are demonically bound or, like this invalid, from those who have not heard the gospel. When He met this man later at the temple, however, He said to him, "See, you are well again. Stop sinning or something worse may happen to you" (John 5:14).

MOVED WITH COMPASSION

The sight of sick people who needed healing moved Jesus' heart with compassion: "When he saw the crowds, he had compassion on them, because they were harassed and helpless, like sheep without a shepherd" (Matt. 9:36). This statement immediately follows a description of His ministry: "Jesus went through all the towns and villages, teaching in their synagogues, preaching the good news of the kingdom and healing every kind of disease and sickness" (v. 35).

His compassion for the people was so great that He told His disciples, "Ask the Lord of the harvest, therefore, to send out workers into his harvest field" (v. 38). The harvest is plentiful, He told them, but the workers are very few to meet such immense human need.

So He sent the Twelve, commissioning them to drive out evil spirits and "to heal every disease and sickness" (Matt. 10:1). Within the limitations of His humanity, Jesus could not minister to every one of the people personally. His love for them was so great that He sent the Twelve to share in the task. Later He sent another seventy-two. The work continued to grow, and more were needed to reach out with the good news of the kingdom and God's healing power.

Before the feeding of the five thousand, we read that Jesus saw the large crowd, "had compassion on them and healed their sick" (Matt. 14:14). When two blind men came to Jesus, He "had compassion on them and touched their eyes. Immediately they received their sight and followed him" (Matt. 20:34).

When Jesus healed the man with leprosy, He was "filled with compassion" (Mark 1:41). This is the same compassion that led Him to feed the multitude and made the father receive with joy the prodigal son.

HE IS STILL THE GOD OF COMPASSION

Is God any less compassionate today? Who would dare to accuse Him of such a thing? Is He compassionate to repentant sinners, but He no longer desires to work miracles and heal people who are sick? If so, He has lost some of His compassion—and that is unthinkable.

Now that Jesus has ascended and is glorified and the Holy Spirit has been given to God's children, *is He not able to express His mercy and compassion more fully rather than less fully?*

Paul certainly knew God as the Father of compassion: "Praise be to the God and Father of our Lord Jesus Christ, the Father of compassion and the God of all comfort, who comforts us in all our troubles" (2 Cor. 1:3–4). He comforts us in *all* our troubles. The word *comfort* in Scripture means not to sympathize but to give strength to the needy one.

Jesus did not sympathize with sick people or support them in their need; *He had compassion on them and healed them.*

His commission to the church is not to sympathize with people who are sick but *to heal them.*

Before giving instructions about how people with illnesses are to be healed, James said, "The Lord is full of compassion and mercy" (James 5:11). He does not change. He is still full of compassion and mercy.

When you understand God's compassion, your faith in Him is enlarged. He is not only *willing* to heal; He *longs* to heal. He is the Lord who delights in mercy and is eager to share His good things with His children.

He showed mercy to Bartimaeus, to the man who had been ill for thirty-eight years, and to *all* who came to Him in sickness.

Jesus has compassion on you.

Jesus wants to show you His mercy.

Jesus does not sympathize with you but desires to heal you.

Jesus sees the work is so great, and His compassion is so immense, that He is sending out laborers today to preach the kingdom and heal people who are sick.

The LORD is gracious and compassionate,
    slow to anger and rich in love.
The LORD is good to all;
    he has compassion on all he has made (Ps. 145:8–9).

14

FAITH AND UNBELIEF

To the man who was brought to Jesus with a "shriveled hand," He said, "'Stretch out your hand.' So he stretched it out and it was completely restored, just as sound as the other" (Matt. 12:13). His opponents used this event as another basis for criticism, for this healing took place on the Sabbath.

"Then they brought him a demon-possessed man who was blind and mute, and Jesus healed him, so that he could both talk and see" (v. 22). This time His enemies claimed He was using demonic powers to drive out other demons. If people do not want to believe, they will invent any number of reasons to excuse their unbelief.

THE POWER OF UNBELIEF

Even Jesus could perform few miracles in His own hometown, Nazareth. Why? Because of the unbelief of the local people: "He could not do any miracles there, except lay his hands on a few sick people and heal them. And he was amazed at their lack of faith" (Mark 6:5–6).

Jesus had been amazed at the faith demonstrated by the Roman centurion. By contrast, He was amazed at the unbelief shown by His own people.

Again the message is clear: *unbelief prevents God from working in the powerful ways He desires.* When shall we stop looking around for reasons why we do not see more healing and face the truth? It is because of our unbelief—unbelief at a personal level, unbelief at the corporate level of the church; unbelief in His love and grace, unbelief in His compassion and mercy; unbelief in all He has accomplished for us on the cross.

Jesus took Peter, James, and John up the Mount of Transfiguration. When they came down, a man approached Jesus; the rest of the disciples had failed to heal his son, who had epilepsy. Jesus did not spare the disciples' feelings: "O unbelieving and perverse generation . . . how long shall I stay with you? How long shall I put up with you?" (Matt. 17:17). They had to face the truth about their failure. The father said to Jesus, "But if you can do anything, take pity on us and help us" (Mark 9:22). Again Jesus detects unbelief: "'If you can?' . . . Everything is possible for him who believes" (Mark 9:23).

When the man with leprosy approached Jesus at the beginning of His ministry, He removed the *if* from the sick man's inquiry—"If you are willing, you can make me clean"—by declaring, "I am willing. Be clean." When the boy's father questions whether Jesus can heal, He is quick to remove the *if* once again.

THE POWER OF FAITH

Everything is possible for him who believes. We need to understand two truths. First, Jesus always healed those with whom He prayed, for He expressed perfect faith in His Father's willingness to heal. Second, nothing is beyond possibility when we put our faith in Jesus. Unbelief, as at Nazareth, prevents God from working in the way He desires.

This is not a popular truth to face. The boy's father had the right attitude: "I do believe; help me overcome my unbelief!" (Mark 9:24). He had a measure of faith or he would not have brought his son for healing in the first place. His conversation with Jesus, however, had revealed the unbelief in his heart. He did not try to hide it or excuse himself for it. He did not try to vindicate himself in any way. Instead he asked Jesus to help him in his unbelief.

What an example for many who struggle to see God's healing power in their own lives or in the lives of others in the church. The quickest way to be rid of unbelief is to recognize it for what it is, confess it as sin, ask for the Lord's forgiveness, and allow Him to speak faith into your heart. It is difficult to receive a word of faith for a particular situation with unrecognized or unconfessed sin lurking beneath the surface.

WHY COULDN'T WE?

Jesus rebuked the evil spirit in the boy and healed him.

Jesus healed *all* who came to Him. The father brought his son to Jesus, but because of His absence while on the Mount of Transfiguration, it was the disciples who had prayed with him instead. So the disciples came to Jesus afterward and said, "Why couldn't we drive it out?" (Matt. 17:19). Why hadn't they been able to heal him? They had presumably prayed with him in the usual way. They were accustomed to seeing success, not failure. So they wanted to know the cause of their failure.

Two gospel accounts seem to record Jesus giving different answers. In fact, He gives the same answer in two different forms. In Matthew, Jesus says, "Because you have so little faith" (17:20). In Mark, He replies, "This kind can come out only by prayer" (9:29).

Jesus never separates prayer from faith. All our praying is to be praying with faith, believing God gives us what we ask. What use is prayer without faith? The disciples must have prayed without faith. They did not believe the victory. No doubt their fault lay in looking at the facts instead of believing the truth. They were more intent on looking at the circumstances than believing their victory over the circumstances.

Jesus forces home the point: "I tell you the truth, if you have faith as small as a mustard seed, you can say to this mountain, 'Move from here to there' and it will move. Nothing will be impossible for you" (Matt. 17:20).

In all their efforts, driving out the evil spirit must have seemed to the disciples like trying to move a mountain. It was not the amount so much as the quality of the faith that counted. It is possible to have a considerable amount of faith in the Lord's ability to heal. What matters is faith in the heart, so that when the need is addressed, the person knows it will be dealt with. When that quality of faith is present, nothing seems impossible.

Jesus says, "Whatever you ask for in prayer, believe that you have received it, and it will be yours" (Mark 11:24). *Whatever! Whatever you ever ask God in prayer, believe you have it. Whenever you ask for anything, believe you have received it.*

DON'T CONDEMN OTHERS

It never helps to say to someone, "You haven't been healed because you don't have enough faith." That statement is usually unloving and condemning. If you are going to minister in love to people, you have a responsibility to build faith in them. You need to speak God's Word to them so that their faith grows.

On the other hand, it is not helpful for some to imagine they are in a place of faith when they are not. If there is unbelief, let it be exposed so that there can be repentance and forgiveness from God, followed by the opportunity for words of faith to be spoken to the heart.

It is not only the faith of the person with the illness that counts but also the faith of those ministering to him. In this incident the lack of faith and authority of those nine disciples was exposed.

How would most people react in a similar situation today? Instead of admitting their lack of faith, they would be more likely to suggest it was not God's purpose to heal that particular boy at that particular time. Perhaps they would also mutter platitudes about God's sovereignty!

Jesus exposes the inadequacy of such explanations. He demonstrates that His Father's purpose *is* to free the boy, despite the lack of faith in His disciples and the limited trust of the lad's father. *God's sovereign will is to heal!*

You may feel in a similar position to the man who said, "I do believe; help me overcome my unbelief!" (Mark 9:24). Jesus will help you as He helped him. He was honest about his need, his lack of faith. If you are honest, God will then forgive and encourage faith in your heart. You will find you are able to receive His Word with faith.

If you feel there have been situations in the past when you have not had faith, do not allow yourself to feel condemned about those occasions. Confess the sin of your unbelief; receive God's forgiveness and know that you are free of all guilt. You are free also to face the future with faith in God, not only to meet your need but to use you to speak faith and healing to others.

Jesus encourages you to pray with faith.
Jesus wants you to speak to mountains and see them moved.
Jesus wants you to believe that whatever you ask the Father in His name, He will give to you.

I do believe; help me overcome my unbelief! (Mark 9:24).

15

THE THIEF

Jesus teaches us that Satan is a thief, the father of lies, the deceiver of God's people. His intention is to steal, destroy, and kill. He wants to steal the physical health of God's people through the sickness and disease with which he has contaminated the Lord's beautiful creation. He wants to destroy faith, causing fear, anxiety, and emotional turmoil in people's lives. He will kill us if he has the opportunity.

One of Satan's greatest triumphs is to cause distress to God's children and then convince them that the fault lies in themselves. Consequently, they accuse themselves and feel utterly condemned instead of recognizing the cause of the problem and rebuking him. Accusation is the devil's business, whether he does it directly or through others.

His second great triumph is to convince people that he does not exist. If people, even churchgoing people, do not know him for what he is, he is free to cause havoc in their lives. Such people then piously ascribe the devil's activities to the will of God!

Satan is the one who opposes the Lord's will and purposes. He destroys; Jesus came to give life in all its fullness. Jesus said, "The thief comes only to steal and kill and destroy; I have come that they may have life, and have it to the full" (John 10:10).

A thief works by stealth so that he cannot be detected. Satan does not come banging on your door telling you he is about to tempt you or mislead you. He uses all his craft to draw your attention away from God and faith in His Word and to yourself—your feelings or circumstances. He has a vested interest in doing that when it comes to healing, for it is he who causes sickness and disease. He is intent on destroying lives spiritually, emotionally, and physically and on bringing division and hatred into relationships.

A person is only deceived when she is convinced she is right although in fact she is wrong. She is not deceived until she commits herself to wrong thinking or activity, believing it to be right.

JOB'S DILEMMA

Job was a blameless and upright man; he feared God and shunned evil. He was prosperous, and he is described as "the greatest man among all the people of the East" (Job 1:3).

When Satan tested his righteousness, faith, and obedience, one disaster after another befell Job, who reflected sadly,

> What I feared has come upon me;
> what I dreaded has happened to me.
> I have no peace, no quietness;
> I have no rest, but only turmoil (Job 3:25–26).

There had been deep inner fear within Job that he would lose his peace, prosperity, and good health. Sickness often begins as a fear, a negative seed planted in a person's mind by Satan. Medical opinion tells us that over 70 percent of physical sickness is psychosomatic; it begins in the mind. Many live in dread of disease, especially cancer, and are not surprised when such an illness is diagnosed after several years of fear. This is the consequence of their negative faith. "I told you so," they say. "I knew it would happen one day. I knew I would get it."

RESIST THE ENEMY

It is better to cut sickness off at its source rather than wait for it to develop. When you have any thought of sickness, resist it immediately in the name of Jesus. If you are alone, you can speak aloud: "I resist that thought in the name of Jesus. I will not have that disease." This is not mind over matter but the spirit over mind and matter.

If you receive the negative suggestion, Satan is quick to follow it with another and then another. Resist the first negative thought. Do not receive the idea of sickness in your spirit. You are to take *every* thought captive for Christ.

There are many Christians who certainly love the Lord but have allowed the enemy to have a stronghold in their minds as far as sickness is concerned. They expect to be ill and often are. They may describe themselves as weak or sickly—hardly a demonstration of faith! They talk more of their symptoms than of the healing power of their Lord. They imagine healing is for others, not for them. They will bear their sickness patiently for the Lord!

He does not call His children to bear sickness. Jesus carried the sicknesses to the cross. We are to patiently bear suffering for the sake of the gospel, but we are not to bear sickness. The believer is to resist the very thought of sickness that comes from the thief, Satan, who loves to steal the health of God's people if he is given opportunity.

Often people blame God for what the enemy does. God does not desire sickness for you, nor does He want you to live expecting to become ill. Through sin and disobedience, you can make yourself vulnerable to the enemy and therefore vulnerable to sickness. You can fail to resist the enemy's thoughts of sickness, but it is not God's purpose to give you a long, painful illness before you die. His best purpose for you is that you will quietly fall asleep in the Lord's arms, having fulfilled your full life span.

DECEIVER OF GOD'S PEOPLE

The devil has deceived many Christians about God's Word concerning healing. He suggests that God does not always want to heal, that He is glorified in sickness, that there is no physical healing in the Atonement. He encourages people to believe that healing is not for today or is only for a favored few.

We should not be surprised by these tactics, for it has always been Satan's business to deny the truth of God's Word or to misuse it so that people are robbed of faith. When he tempted Eve in the Garden of Eden, she told Satan that God had said, "You must not eat fruit from the tree that is in the middle of the garden, and you must not touch it, or you will die" (Gen. 3:3).

Satan immediately contradicted God. "You will not surely die," he said to Eve (v. 4). After she and Adam had eaten, they discovered that what God said was the truth. Whatever denies His Word is ultimately of the devil.

To believe the thoughts that deny the truth robs people of the truth that is able to set them free and at the same time honors the one whose business is to encourage disbelief. When Jesus was tempted in the wilderness by Satan, three times He answered the devil with the words: "It is written . . ." (Matt. 4:4–10). *The devil has no answer to the truth that is written— when God's people believe it.* So he attempts anything to encourage us to question or doubt what God says.

The quickest way to deal with the devil is to believe God,

to exercise your authority over the evil one, the authority given to you as a child of God's kingdom. "I have given you authority to trample on snakes and scorpions and to overcome all the power of the enemy; nothing will harm you," Jesus said (Luke 10:19).

JOB'S ANSWER

It was the Lord's word that came to Job that led to his restoration to health and well-being. There was no point in Job or anyone else blaming God for what was happening: "The LORD said to Job: 'Will the one who contends with the Almighty correct him? Let him who accuses God answer him!'" (Job 40:1–2). The Lord makes it clear to His servant that He is the God who creates and He is the one who is able to do what He wills and desires with His creation. As the Lord was to say to Isaiah, it is not for the clay to tell the potter what to do (Isa. 29:16).

Job's response to the Lord is important: "I know that you can do all things; no plan of yours can be thwarted" (42:2). Job prayed for his friends who had given him bad advice, and then the Lord made him prosperous again and gave him twice as much as he had before. The Lord blessed the latter part of Job's life more than the former. Having brought Job through the horrendous trials he endured, the Lord greatly prospered him.

FORGIVE YOUR FALSE COMFORTERS

Notice that Job had to forgive those who had ill-advised him, telling him that his sickness was justified, and pray for them before restoration took place.

Have you been taught in the past that your sickness was sent to you from God? If so, forgive those who told you such things.

Have you been taught that God is glorified in sickness? Forgive those who said so and pray for them.

Have you been taught to submit to sickness as God's will for you? Again, forgive those who misguidedly taught you what opposes His Word.

Forgive all those who have been as Job's comforters to you. Like Job, cast yourself on the love, grace, and mercy of the Lord almighty, who is your loving Father—and know it is His purpose to heal and restore you.

It may be that you have to ask the Lord to forgive you for doubting or questioning His words, for listening to the reasoning of people or the lies inspired by the enemy. He is ready to forgive and longs to see you exercising faith in His Word.

Even when experience seems to contradict the Word, believe what God says.
God's words are eternal and will never change.
Your experience can easily be changed by faith in God's Word.
Do not allow Satan to rob you of faith in God's Word.

The thief comes only to steal and kill and destroy; I have come that they may have life, and have it to the full (John 10:10).

16

AUTHORITY OVER SATAN

Jesus spoke with such authority that He had command not only over sickness but also over the demonic powers that caused sickness and produced chaos and havoc in people's lives: "When evening came, many who were demon-possessed were brought to him, and he drove out the spirits with a word and healed all the sick" (Matt. 8:16). His words, spoken with authority, brought immediate deliverance to people who were brought to Him.

AUTHORITY OF THE BELIEVER

Jesus gave His disciples similar authority: "He called his twelve disciples to him and gave them authority to drive out evil spirits and to heal every disease and sickness" (Matt. 10:1). He told the seventy-two He sent later, "I have given you authority to trample on snakes and scorpions and to overcome all the power of the enemy" (Luke 10:19).

Later still He makes it clear this authority is extended to all believers: "And these signs will accompany those who believe: In my name they will drive out demons... they will place their hands on sick people, and they will get well" (Mark 16:17–18).

We will discuss deliverance at greater length later. However, it is necessary to understand now the authority God has given you as a believer and the power that can be released into the events of your life through the proper use of your words.

There is no deliverance ministry in the New Testament that is separate from the total ministry of healing seen in Jesus' ministry and given to believers. Anybody exercising a ministry of healing comes to appreciate the demonic forces that can be at work in mental, emotional, and physical sickness. To believers, Jesus gives authority over all these forces.

EXERCISE YOUR AUTHORITY

You do not have to adopt the attitude that the devil has you in his grip, that he is tormenting you and there is nothing you can do about it. As a Christian, you are in Jesus' grip, not Satan's. God has transformed you from the kingdom of darkness and brought you into His kingdom of light. When light meets darkness, the light prevails.

You can tell the devil to take his hands off your life—and you don't have to be polite in the way you do so. *You belong to Jesus, not to him. He has no right to plague you, no control over your life unless you surrender that control to him.* You certainly don't want to do that!

You are not a person to surrender to sickness as the will of God. Use your authority against the one who wants to steal your health from you, the one who is a thief and robber. You have power over him. Speak to that mountain of need in your life, and command it to be thrown into the sea. Jesus tells you to do so.

After the disciples woke Jesus when they were afraid of drowning in the storm, He "rebuked the winds and the waves, and it was completely calm" (Matt. 8:26). But He also rebuked the disciples for their lack of faith: "You of little faith, why are you so afraid?"

Like Jesus, when we exercise faith, we speak to the situation with authority. We speak in the name of Jesus. We speak as He would speak; we believe what He would believe in that same situation. We do not view the matter with fear, which is the opposite of faith. When we fear, we are unlikely to speak with authority. Even if our initial reaction is to fear, as we begin to speak to the situation in faith, we find authority increasing.

How does Jesus view sickness? He does not tremble at the thought of it; He exercises authority over it. That is how He wants you to respond to sickness or any other attack of the enemy on your well-being.

When the demon-possessed men met Jesus, He commanded the demons to leave them with a single word: "Go!" (Matt. 8:32). He spoke the word with faith and authority. Jesus knew the demons must obey Him.

Not all sickness is caused by evil spirits, but some sicknesses do have a direct relation to demonic powers, which are in submission to Satan and which he uses to bring much misery into people's lives. But the power and authority of Jesus are much greater than any of those powers of darkness, and the power and authority that God gives you as a believer are greater than those demonic forces.

> *You do not need to allow the enemy to steal your health from you!*
>
> *You can speak to the sickness in your life and command it to be moved in the name of Jesus.*
>
> *Faith is not a feeling but is expressed in what you say and do.*
>
> *So speak in faith with the authority God gives you: "Sickness—go in the name of Jesus!" Praise God for His victory.*

I have given you authority. . . to overcome all the power of the enemy (Luke 10:19).

||||||||||||||||||||||||||||||||||||||||||||||||

Part Three

PRAYING FOR YOUR HEALING

||||||||||||||||||||||||||||||||||||||||||||||||

17

PRAY IN HIS NAME

How can we relate to the suggestion that if we have faith in Jesus, we will do similar things and greater things than He did? Such an idea can be reality only if we learn to pray with faith.

Immediately after making this amazing statement, Jesus promises, "And I will do whatever you ask in my name, so that the Son may bring glory to the Father" (John 14:13).

You can be sure that Jesus wants to answer your prayers of faith "so that the Son may bring glory to the Father." This is the motive throughout Jesus' ministry: He didn't come to glorify Himself; He came to glorify His Father. He came to speak the words of His Father, to proclaim the works of His Father, to do the will of His Father. He knows it will please the Father to see faith in the hearts of His children—faith that will release His power, His healing, and His provision into their lives.

IN MY NAME

What an amazing promise: "I will do whatever you ask in my name"! The key phrase is "in my name." What does it mean to pray in Jesus' name? "In Jesus' name" is not a phrase to tack on to the end of your prayers so that everyone knows it is time to say "Amen." Neither is it a magic phrase that will ensure that the one praying will receive immediately the desired answer.

To pray in the name of Jesus is to pray as Jesus would pray, to see the situation as He would see it, to believe what He would believe, to ask what He would ask, to expect what He would expect, to believe the truth rather than the facts.

We have the same Father as Jesus. The same Spirit who lived in Him lives in us. All the resources of God's heavenly kingdom are available to us, as they were available to Him.

Jesus gives us the power of the Holy Spirit so that in any situation in which we are placed, we can learn to pray in His name. We can look at the situation from God's perspective.

We tend to look at needs from a human perspective, believing the facts rather than the truth of what God is able to do to change those facts. When a doctor diagnoses a terminal sickness, the more we look at the need, the more desperate the situation becomes. It sometimes requires considerable effort to take our eyes off the problem and look to Jesus, who can speak faith to our hearts for the need. This is particularly difficult in a hospital when people are looking to the next pill, injection, or doctor's round rather than to the Lord.

God's resources and power are unlimited. When you look at things from God's perspective, you realize sickness is no problem for Him. It is not difficult for God to heal cancer, to straighten twisted limbs, or to heal the brokenhearted. But He does want faith to work with. To have God's divine perspective on your life is to know that in His love He wants to meet your needs and that in His power He is able to do so.

BELIEVE THE PROMISES

Sometimes we have to acknowledge that we do not have the necessary faith because we do not believe the tremendous prayer promises that Jesus gives us: "You may ask me for anything in my name, and I will do it" (John 14:14). We imagine that some things are beyond His love or power, or we pray tentatively rather than with conviction because we doubt His willingness to give to us personally. We know what He is able to do but doubt His willingness to do it.

Jesus said, "You did not choose me, but I chose you and appointed you to go and bear fruit—fruit that will last. *Then the Father will give you whatever you ask in my name*" (John 15:16, italics mine). The Father has chosen you. He wants you to be fruitful in His purposes. And He wants to give you whatever you ask in Jesus' name.

Let that truth ring in your heart. *God, your Father, wants to give you whatever you ask in the name of His Son.* He wants you to dare to ask what Jesus would ask, believe what Jesus would believe, pray as Jesus would pray. He longs to see such faith in your heart.

Dare to do that now. How would Jesus pray about that present need? He would not pray, "If it be Your will..." When it comes to healing, that is a faith-killing statement. God has declared clearly that it is His will to heal all, and He made provision for healing on the cross.

To pray, "If it be Your will...," for healing is an admission that you doubt the revelation of God's Word. Jesus never questioned His Father's will to heal; He never taught us to pray, "If it be Your will."

Quite the opposite. He was never vague about what He believed the outcome of His prayer would be. He was never halfhearted or double-minded in His asking.

He was bold, authoritative, and full of faith. And that confidence is what He wants from you!

You have the privilege and ability to pray in the name of Jesus and know that the Father wants to give you whatever you ask: "I tell you the truth, my Father will give you whatever you ask in my name. Until now you have not asked for anything in my name. Ask and you will receive, and your joy will be complete" (John 16:23–24).

> *You know the will of God regarding healing.*
> *You have the privilege of praying in Jesus' name.*
> *Ask, and you will receive.*
> *Your joy will be full.*

And I will do whatever you ask in my name, so that the Son may bring glory to the Father (John 14:13).

18

HAVE FAITH IN GOD

Jesus wants to encourage you; He wants you to understand that God is the God of grace, who loves you and wants to heal you and pour His riches into your life. As He did His first disciples, Jesus wants to teach you to pray the prayer of faith.

Jesus indicates that the first step is to "have faith in God" (Mark 11:22). Although we are talking about this prayer of faith within the context of healing, the principles that Jesus teaches are true when praying for anything else, when seeking the answer to any other kind of need.

WHERE DO YOU PUT YOUR FAITH?

That the disciples needed to have faith in God seems self-evident at first. Why should Jesus say what was so obvious? Because He knew those disciples well, and He knows we are prone to make the same mistakes they did. It is possible to put your faith in your symptoms, in which case you will believe in healing only after those symptoms have disappeared. If you experience pain or discomfort, you believe you have not been healed.

Your faith is where you put the emphasis in your life. Faith isn't a feeling or a sensation; it is trusting God. Faith or unbelief is therefore demonstrated in the things you say and do. You don't have faith until you put God's Word into operation. Faith believes His truth is able to change the facts; it does not concentrate on the facts themselves.

When Jesus came toward the disciples walking on the water, it would not have been enough for Peter to say, "I believe that I have heard the Lord tell me to come and to walk on the water to Him." When Peter heard Jesus say, "Come," he had to exercise faith by actually stepping out of the boat and on to the water. His faith at that moment was in Jesus to enable him to do it; and he walked on the water. It was when he began to doubt because he was conscious of his circumstances, of water under his feet and the wind blowing his hair, that he began to sink and had to cry out, "Lord, save me!" Jesus drew him to Himself and said to him, "You of little faith . . . why did you doubt?" (Matt. 14:31). Peter had the faith to step on to the water, but when he took his eyes off Jesus and concentrated on the circumstances, he found himself in real trouble.

It is possible to believe your symptoms, your feelings, or your fears. Much fear is associated with sickness: Will I die? Is it a terminal sickness? Is it cancer?

Satan likes to sow seeds of fear in the mind, and much physical and emotional sickness begins when such fears are heeded and believed.

Jesus directs you to this great truth: *your faith needs to be in God, not in your situation, not in your circumstances, not in what you feel, not in who you are but in who He is.*

FIX YOUR EYES ON JESUS

The first principle to learn about praying with faith is to take your eyes off yourself—your need, your circumstances, your feelings, your symptoms—and fix them on God. Where you fix your gaze is evidence of where you place your faith: "Let us fix our eyes on Jesus, the author and perfecter of our faith" (Heb. 12:2).

Your faith in Jesus is determined by your understanding of who He is. He is loving and gracious, compassionate and merciful. He wants to give to you, to share Himself with you, to speak faith to your heart, and to heal you. He has declared His great love for you by the sacrifice of His life so that you may be able to experience His forgiveness and healing: "And my God will meet all your needs according to his glorious riches in Christ Jesus" (Phil. 4:19).

Your focus needs to be upon the glorious riches that are yours in Christ. God has blessed you in Christ with every spiritual blessing in the heavenly places. Because you belong to Christ by virtue of your new birth, you can pray with faith, reaching up to heaven and appropriating whatever God has given you in Jesus.

Faith releases the activity of God and His provision of healing into your life. *The only way your faith can be enlarged is to look away from yourself and your need. Look to Jesus, look at His Word, because faith comes from hearing that Word, not mentally assenting to its truth but hearing and believing it in your heart.* Read the prayer promises over and over again, allowing the Spirit to witness the truth of them to you personally. Look at all the Scriptures about healing, and be encouraged by the fact that Jesus healed all who came to Him.

A FATAL ERROR

It is possible to put your faith in a medical prognosis. Diagnosis can provide important information, but the prognosis given by the doctor takes no account of what God is able to do.

Imagine that two Christians, both born-again men, receive an identical prognosis from the doctor: they have cancer and can expect to live for only three months. The first receives the news passively: "Thank you, doctor. Can nothing be done?" When he is told that medical treatment would be of no avail, he leaves the doctor's office believing he is under sentence of death. He has received the cancer in his spirit in addition to having it in his body.

Subsequently, he may pray because he realizes God is able to heal. But he has a real faith battle on his hands because of the double healing he needs. He believes not only the cancer but the doctor's prognosis.

The second man hears an identical medical verdict, but his spontaneous response to the news is different: "No, I will not die within three months because by the stripes of Jesus I have been healed." He meets the situation with active, positive, and definite faith. He refuses to accept or believe the fact of the cancer in his spirit—although he knows the fact of it in his body.

Whereas the first man may or may not receive healing as he struggles to come to a place of faith, the second man is in a much stronger faith position. It is very important to realize we are talking here not about glib formulas but about genuine faith attitudes that reflect what is in the individual's heart.

A WELLSPRING OF LIFE

The Lord wants you to live by faith in the revelation of His Word so that when any unexpected problem arises, there is a spontaneous response of active faith from you. You live with the truth of His Word in your spirit and refuse to receive anything negative there.

If you have already received a negative idea or attitude in your spirit, what can you do about it? Confess the sin and ask the Lord to forgive you. His cleansing removes the guilt of the negativity in your spirit. Stand firm against those unbelieving thoughts and attitudes. Rebuke them, for they have no right to influence you as a child of God. Ask Him, then, to speak a word of revelation to your spirit by the Holy Spirit, who lives in you. Faith comes from hearing the Word of God spoken to your heart by the Holy Spirit.

Receive the positive truth of His Word into your spirit. These are words of spirit and life, of truth and healing:

> My son, pay attention to what I say;
>   listen closely to my words.
> Do not let them out of your sight,
>   keep them within your heart;
> for they are life to those who find them
>   and health to a man's whole body (Prov. 4:20–22).

Once you have received those words in your heart, hold on to them; they will begin to influence your thinking, your emotions, and even your body. When you are tempted to doubt because you may still be conscious of symptoms, hold on in faith to the words God has spoken to you. Believe the truth that is able to change the facts: "Above all else, guard your heart, for it is the wellspring of life" (v. 23).

The truth in your heart will be a wellspring of life to your body. How important, therefore, to have God's words stored up within you. The Holy Spirit is then able to take them and speak them to your heart, the right words for the right occasion.

> *Have faith in God.*
> *Fix your eyes on God's words; don't let them out of your sight.*
> *Keep His words stored in your heart.*
> *They are health to your whole body.*
> *Guard your heart; it is the wellspring of life.*

My words . . . are life to those who find them and health to a man's whole body (Prov. 4:22).

19

MOVING MOUNTAINS

When Jesus says, "I tell you the truth . . . ," He not only wants to underline the significance of what He is about to say; He also knows His words will be met with unbelief. Every time Jesus spoke He told the truth; sometimes the truth is hard to accept because it seems incredible to us.

Jesus said, "I tell you the truth, if anyone says to this mountain, 'Go, throw yourself into the sea,' and does not doubt in his heart but believes that what he says will happen, it will be done for him" (Mark 11:23). When praying the prayer of faith, stage one is to have faith in God. Stage two is to speak to the mountain and command it to move.

SPEAK TO YOUR PROBLEMS

How often do you speak to your problems? This is a question I often ask people, and the great majority admit they never speak to them. Yet this is what Jesus tells you to do. If you don't do things the way He directs, you shouldn't complain if you don't obtain the results you want when praying to Him.

When Jesus says to speak to the mountain, He does not intend for you to stand at the foot of Mount Everest and say, "Everest, be moved in the name of Jesus!" That is clearly ridiculous. He is not referring to rocky mountains; He is talking about need, about problems that arise in the daily events of your life and that form a barrier in front of you.

These are the problems that impede your progress, trying to prevent you from moving forward in God's purposes. Some are tempted to find a way around the need; others try to climb the mountain, often imagining they are pleasing the Lord with their strenuous efforts.

Jesus tells you to address the need—to speak to the problem and command it to be moved. You do not have to move it, but you do have to speak to it. This requires another step in faith: *When you speak, believe that the mountain will be moved.*

Sickness can be seen as a mountain that needs to be moved. There is no point in saying to your need, "Sickness, would you please depart from my life if it's not too much trouble?" That is hardly speaking with authority and conviction in the way Jesus did. When you speak in such ways, there is obviously no faith in your heart to believe the sickness is going to be moved. You need to command the problem, "Sickness, in the name of Jesus, move!" Exhibit the faith of the centurion who knew that when he issued orders, they had to be obeyed. *You speak in the name of Jesus, with His authority, which is greater than any sickness.* Remember how often He healed with a word.

THE MOUNTAIN WILL BE MOVED

Nothing is impossible for God; nothing is impossible for those who have faith in Him. You are able, in the name of Jesus, to address that problem and command it to move.

Moving mountains results from the faith attitude in the hearts of believers. They realize that they do not have to live with problems that are not God's will for them. The ones who speak to mountains understand that as Christians they are in a spiritual battle. They are not to receive passively what the forces of opposition try to lay upon them. They understand that the Lord does not create these needs and then tell His children to command their removal. He delights in the fighting faith attitude that inspires believers to resist the problems and see them moved.

Jesus does not say you need a great amount of faith; you need only a speck of the right quality of faith—faith that expects results: "I tell you the truth, if you have faith as small as a mustard seed, you can say to this mountain, 'Move from here to there' and it will move. Nothing will be impossible for you" (Matt. 17:20).

You cannot move the problem, but God will when you speak to it in faith. *You are to speak to the mountain, not live with the problem.* Your responsibility as a Christian is not to help people live with their mountains but to lead them to the kind of faith where they can speak to the problem and command it to move in the name of Jesus. And Jesus promises that it will be moved.

> *Are you living with a mountain of need? If so, speak to that need and command it to move.*
>
> *Do not doubt in your heart; believe that what you say will happen.*
>
> *The words you speak with faith and authority are powerful.*
>
> *Maintain that positive attitude until the mountain has been removed and cast into the sea, sunk without trace and never to be seen again.*

I tell you the truth, if anyone says to this mountain, "Go, throw yourself into the sea," and does not doubt in his heart but believes that what he says will happen, it will be done for him (Mark 11:23).

20

BELIEVE YOU HAVE RECEIVED

Jesus says, "Therefore I tell you, whatever you ask for in prayer, believe that you have received it, and it will be yours" (Mark 11:24). This is stage three of the prayer of faith. You have put your faith in God; you have spoken to the mountain; now speak to the Lord. It doesn't have to be a long prayer. We will not be heard for our many words, Jesus said. When you have faith, you will be amazed at how few words you need.

THE TEST OF FAITH

How do you know you are in a place of genuine faith? When you pray and believe you have received your answer, you know in your heart the matter is resolved, even if there is no visible justification for such faith. You have met with God, and the matter is dealt with.

Remember the difference between hope and faith. Hope says that something will happen in the future; faith says, "I have received it already," even when there is no visible evidence for such faith. Jesus says "Believe that you have received it, and it will be yours." He doesn't say it will be yours *immediately*, but He does promise it will be yours.

THE TIME LAPSE

Sometimes when you are in the place of faith, you have the answer immediately; your healing happens instantaneously. On other occasions, there is a time lapse between the prayer of faith and the moment when the healing is actually manifested. That time lapse can be a great test of faith, in which you might experience times of doubt.*

There is an important difference between unbelief and doubt. Before God brought you into the place of faith, you were in unbelief. Once you have received faith for the answer to your need, you may have times of doubt. Unbelief is an

---

*In *Anything You Ask*, I explain that some answers seem to come like rockets—fast, instantaneous answers that are right on target. Other answers seem like tortoises, slowly progressing toward the believer. The danger with the tortoise answers is that the Christian can give up instead of inheriting the promises by faith with patience. That lack of perseverance demonstrates there was a lack of the faith that believes the answer is already received.

absence of faith. Doubt momentarily questions the faith you have received. When you doubt in that way, the Holy Spirit quickly brings you back to the position of faith because you lose the peace that comes with trusting God. You can pray, "Lord, I'm sorry for doubting You and Your word to me, and I praise and thank You for the answer of my need."

I am not talking about trying to make yourself believe you have received your answer when there has been no genuine faith. I mean that *once you have received heart revelation, you can quickly come back to faith* because deep in your heart you *know* you have received your answer. You know God has spoken and He is faithful.

REVELATION IN YOUR SPIRIT

Someone may ask you how you know God has answered you when there is no visible evidence to substantiate that. There is no reasonable answer to such a question because we are talking about revelation received in your spirit, not coming to a mental or an emotional assessment of the situation. When Jesus has spoken to you personally by the Spirit, you know the reality of that, and nothing can shake you from your conviction of what He has said. This sounds very subjective, and it is. The great men and women of prayer call this the *inner witness* of the Spirit. There is no way to define it. You simply know when you have received it.

Christians would find their prayers more powerful and effective if they spent more time seeking the Lord, listening to Him in His Word and by the Spirit, so that they know personally this inner witness.

There are many situations in which I do not have immediate faith that the need is met. I know in my head that it has been, that by the stripes of Jesus I am healed, and that every need is met in the glorious riches that are mine in Christ.

Knowing these things in my mind is not believing them in my heart, applying them to the particular situation before me. Therefore, I have to spend time with the Lord, confessing any unbelief, praying in the Spirit, until I have the conviction in my heart that says, *It is done. I know God has undertaken the matter.* I can rejoice and be glad in His goodness.

Is this not open to abuse or misunderstanding? Can people not be mistaken in what they believe? All of us can be mistaken at times but not about the inner witness of the Spirit. When we receive this inner witness, we *know* what Jesus is saying; we *know* what Jesus will do. If for a moment we doubt or question that, we quickly become very uncomfortable, for we are mentally arguing with what we know in our spirits.

TIME TO RECEIVE

You need to give yourself time in which to receive healing from the Lord. It is easy to spend considerable time asking and give yourself little opportunity to receive. The emphasis needs to be the other way around. Once you have come to a place of revelation, be still and allow the Spirit to come upon you to give you the healing for which you now believe.

You can do this by quietly sitting on your own, waiting on the Lord and knowing that His hand is upon you and that His healing power is flowing into your life. Many find it helpful to pray with others, to use the laying on of hands or anointing. Whatever method is used, the Holy Spirit is the agent through whom God gives His healing. You need to believe, therefore, that at the moment of receiving the laying on of hands or of being anointed, the Spirit is coming upon you and you are receiving your answer.

Then you can be thankful, whether your healing happens instantaneously or whether the Lord initiates a healing process at that time. Certainly, there is no need to be deterred from receiving ministry on a number of occasions until the healing is complete.

It is an integral part of faith to believe you are able to receive. Give yourself time to do so.

As I have prayed with people, I have discovered how important it is to wait for the Spirit to come upon the person; then she knows she is receiving. If nothing is happening at first, we can seek wisdom as to why that is.

Of course, the person is encouraged because she has met with the Lord. But I often impress on people that they need to go on meeting with Him, continuing to receive from Him daily in their own prayer times. It is far more beneficial to meet with the Lord than to concentrate on symptoms and doubt the reality of the healing that is taking place.

Faith is not a cold, academic act of the mind and will; it leads to a personal encounter with the God of love. He communicates this love by the Holy Spirit. So allow the Spirit to come upon you and fill you with His healing power.

THE DOUBLE-MINDED PERSON

James says, "When he asks, he must believe and not doubt, because he who doubts is like a wave of the sea, blown and tossed by the wind. That man should not think he will receive anything from the Lord; he is a double-minded man, unstable in all he does" (James 1:6–8).

The man who has received a revelation of faith may be tempted to doubt and to question what he has heard, but he does not receive those doubts. He knows they conflict with the Word of God, and so he rejects them. That is why it is so important to keep your eyes on the truth of God's Word and not on the facts. His truth is able to change the facts.

The double-minded woman cannot expect to receive anything from the Lord because she vacillates between the facts and the truth; first she believes one and then the other. There is no true inner witness of the Spirit.

PATIENCE

The writer of Hebrews says, "We do not want you to become lazy, but to imitate those who through faith and patience inherit what has been promised" (Heb. 6:12). Patience goes with genuine faith. You cannot hurry God; to receive His words of promise in your heart is enough, for you know that if God has spoken to you, He will certainly keep His word.

Abraham is again an example to us. He inherited God's promises by faith *with patience*: "And so after waiting patiently, Abraham received what was promised" (Heb. 6:15). He kept his attention on what God had said, not on the physical circumstances:

Without weakening in his faith, he faced the fact that his body was as good as dead—since he was about a hundred years old—and that Sarah's womb was also dead. *Yet he did not waver through unbelief regarding the promise of God, but was strengthened in his faith and gave glory to God, being fully persuaded that God had power to do what he had promised* (Rom. 4:19–21, italics mine).

The period of waiting strengthened Abraham's faith and trust in God instead of weakening it. He knew he had heard the Lord—and God does not lie. He is faithful to His promises.

You do not need a word of revelation to know that God desires to heal you; that He does is clear from Scripture. You do need revelation to know that you have received what He promised. Be like those who, Jesus says, with a noble and good heart "hear the word, retain it, and by persevering produce a crop" (Luke 8:15).

> *Your God is faithful.*
> *The Spirit desires to bring His promises to your heart.*
> *Believe you have received your answer.*
> *Inherit what is promised by faith with patience.*

Therefore I tell you, whatever you ask for in prayer, believe that you have received it, and it will be yours (Mark 11:24).

21

FORGIVE

When describing how to pray with faith, Jesus said, "And when you stand praying, if you hold anything against anyone, forgive him, so that your Father in heaven may forgive you your sins" (Mark 11:25). Sickness is of the devil; he is the thief who "comes only to steal and kill and destroy" (John 10:10). He loves to steal your health, and he will kill you if he is given the opportunity.

Sin provides him with the opportunities he desires. Not all sickness is the direct consequence of sin, but unforgiven sin can prevent a person from receiving the healing God wants to give. It is important to keep very short accounts with God. When you do sin, turn back to Him immediately and ask for

His forgiveness. Whatever you do directly against God or others needs His forgiveness.

FORGIVE OTHERS

It is equally important to forgive any who have wronged you. Failure to do so means God will not forgive you: "For if you forgive men when they sin against you, your heavenly Father will also forgive you. But if you do not forgive men their sins, your Father will not forgive your sins" (Matt. 6:14–15).

Jesus told the parable of the unmerciful servant to impress upon people how important it is to forgive others. The servant was forgiven an enormous debt by his master but then had a fellow servant thrown into prison because of the paltry sum he was owed by the fellow servant. When the master discovered the servant to whom he had shown such great mercy had himself been unmerciful, he told him: " 'You wicked servant . . . I canceled all that debt of yours because you begged me to. Shouldn't you have had mercy on your fellow servant just as I had on you?' In anger his master turned him over to the jailers . . . until he should pay back all he owed" (Matt. 18:32–34).

Jesus warned, "This is how my heavenly Father will treat each of you unless you forgive your brother from your heart" (v. 35).

UNFORGIVENESS CAUSES DISEASE

Disease is dis-ease. Physical dis-ease often has spiritual and emotional causes. Hatred, bitterness, resentment, anger, frustration, and other pent-up emotions are ultimately going to find expression in a person's body. The body will scream out in protest at the tension within. Tense or frightened people often suffer from stomach disorders; anxious people from ulcers; contentious and fractious people from arthritis, bone disease, aching joints, and aching backs. This is not to say that all stomach disease is caused by tension or that all arthritis is a result of resentment and bitterness. But it seems that often there is a correlation between these things.

There is little point in coming to the Lord with a physical need, saying, "Lord, heal my arthritis," or "Lord, heal my weak stomach," when there is an underlying cause that needs to be dealt with. The physical condition may be your principal concern, but the Lord wants you to be whole. If He were to take away the symptoms without dealing with the cause, it would be only a matter of time before you would experience a return of the disease.

Weeds grow very readily in a garden and need to be rooted out. If only the top of the weed, which is visible, is removed, the root remains in the ground. The weed will continue to grow and inevitably will appear above ground again. The only way to deal effectively with it is to remove the root.

This is one of the reasons why people can sometimes receive healing when others pray with them, but subsequently, they experience a return of the symptoms. The Lord has honored the faith of those who prayed, but the root cause has not been dealt with.

God does not want to deal with the symptoms alone; He wants to deal with the cause. He wants to heal your body, soul, and spirit.

When Jesus healed the ten men with leprosy, only one came back to give thanks to God. Jesus said that the man was made whole; he wasn't simply healed of his leprosy, but he was made whole spiritually as well. In that one man, God was able to do a thorough and deep work that was not done in the other nine, even though their physical disease was healed.

MORE DIFFICULT FOR CHRISTIANS?

Christians are often perplexed at the way nonbelievers some-times receive healing of physical needs from God in response to prayer while believers find it more difficult to receive. Those who are not Christians are not to be envied. Even if their physical condition is healed, they remain lost and in great need spiritually. God has honored the faith of those who prayed for them, but when dealing with His own children, He wants to do a thorough job, beginning with the spirit and working outward through the soul and body. With non-Christians, He may start with the body. The healing of the lives of non-Christians is incomplete, however, if they do not allow the Lord to touch their spirits, cleansing them of sins and drawing them into a right relationship with God and others.

The Lord will use the opportunities given Him when we seek Him for the healing of physical sickness. At such times He points out to us things in our lives He may have been wanting to deal with for some time: areas of disobedience, sin that has made us vulnerable, or wrong relationships that need to be put right. No longer can we avoid the impact of what He has been saying, especially about being willing to forgive others, not bearing any grudges or holding on to any re-sentment.

When you refuse to forgive someone, it seems as if the windows of heaven are closed in your face. If God hasn't forgiven you your sins, it is very difficult for you to receive anything from Him. These words are always relevant: "Forgive us our trespasses as we forgive those who trespass against us."

RELATIONSHIPS

The Holy Spirit will certainly convince you of wrong relationships if you listen to His voice; you won't have to go digging and delving into the past to discover them. You can pray, "Lord, please show me the things about me and my relationships with others that You want to deal with." He will do so because it is part of His purpose to do so.

Perhaps you haven't been loving toward some people; perhaps you haven't given to them or served them in the ways God has asked of you. You may have held on to a deep grudge or hurt for years but have never associated your physical disease with that resentment.

The Lord may bring to your mind events from childhood. You may realize you have always felt bitter toward one of your parents, toward a brother or sister, or toward someone at school who hurt you. You may be resentful toward somebody at work who has caused you great irritation or toward someone who has swindled you, leaving deep hurt and bitterness. In all these situations the Lord says to forgive. You are to forgive because you aren't in a position to do anything else. You come to the Lord with all your sins, and you expect Him to forgive you again and again; He is willing to do so because of His love for you. So His word to you is that even if someone sins against you seven times a day, you are to continue to forgive the person.

Forgiveness is an attitude of the heart. It is best to be in an attitude of forgiveness before the other person apologizes and even if the person never does so. A wrong reaction not only leaves a bitter relationship but also can cause untold spiritual harm to you.

Peter asked Jesus how many times he was to forgive his brother. He suggested seven times as the maximum. Jesus replied that he was to forgive seventy times seven, an endless number of times. Forgive, forgive, forgive, forgive, and go on forgiving. Failure to do so will result in storing up trouble for yourself:

Do not judge, and you will not be judged. Do not condemn, and you will not be condemned. Forgive, and you will be forgiven. Give, and it will be given to you. A good measure, pressed down, shaken together and running over, will be poured into your lap. For with the measure you use, it will be measured to you (Luke 6:37–38).

Forgiveness is also an act of the will; you *decide* to forgive. The enemy tried to encourage people to imagine they are unable to forgive because of their negative feelings. But when the decision to forgive is made, it is not long before the feelings change. This is another indication as to how unwise it is to be ruled by your feelings.

It is God's purpose for you to forgive others.
It is in your own best interests to do so.
Learn to live with an attitude of forgiveness.
When others hurt or offend you, forgive them immediately
so that resentment does not build up within you.

And when you stand praying, if you hold anything against anyone, forgive him, so that your Father in heaven may forgive you your sins (Mark 11:25).

|||||||||||||||||||||||||||||||||||||||||||||||||||||

Part Four

RECEIVING YOUR
HEALING

|||||||||||||||||||||||||||||||||||||||||||||||||||||

22

BE SPECIFIC

This is a good point at which to summarize so that you can see clearly how to prepare yourself to receive healing from Jesus. Faith is not demonstrated by having a casual attitude—"Lord, I have this need; please heal me"—or by going to a service saying, "I hope something will happen this week; if not, I will try again next week." Healing does not come through hoping for the best. When we come to the Lord with faith in His Word, we can always expect healing to happen as long as we have come in the right way, knowing we are right with God and with others.

Here is a very simple pattern for receiving healing from the Lord or for ministering healing to others. This is a pattern, not a law. These are principles that will help us to receive what God certainly wants to give.

PREPARATION

Come to Jesus humbly and honestly, confessing your sins and asking for His forgiveness. Remember those people who came to Jesus crying, "Lord, have mercy on us!" God wants to heal you although you can never deserve healing. He is the Lord of compassion and mercy. Because He loves you, He wants to give to you, to see His covenant promises fulfilled in your life. To be able to receive His healing, say from your heart, "Lord, forgive me."

Vague prayers receive vague answers; specific prayers receive specific answers. Don't be vague when you pray; always be specific. That is important in confession of sin as well as the prayer of faith. "Lord Jesus, please forgive me all my sins, Amen" is easy to say but does not necessarily indicate that there is real determination to turn away from particular sins and not return to them. It is possible to ask God to forgive sins because it is general knowledge that they are wrong in His sight but without any true awareness as to how deeply grievous to Him those sins are.

Be specific about the particular sins you want Him to forgive and know the truth of His Word: "If we confess our sins, he is faithful and just and will forgive us our sins and purify us from all unrighteousness" (1 John 1:9). If God did not forgive you, He would not be faithful to His Word. When God forgives, He cleanses you from everything that is unrighteous. You are then restored to a state of righteousness; you are put right with Him and so are able to receive anything from Him that He is able to give to you. Unforgiven sin is like a great wall that separates you from God; forgiveness removes the wall and makes it possible for you to receive from Him.

So come humbly and honestly to the Lord your healer. You may find it helpful to spend some time quietly so you can write down what needs to be brought to the Lord in confession, including the wrong heart attitudes, lack of forgiveness, resentment, or hatred toward somebody else.

Do what the Scripture says and examine yourself, but do it without becoming introspective. It is having faith in God's promises that will produce healing, not discovering every sin you have ever committed. You are asking Him to show you whatever could stand in the way of receiving healing.

You are not only bringing your sickness to Him; you are bringing yourself, and you are saying, "Forgive me my sins as I forgive those who sin against me."

FEED ON THE PROMISES

Spend time receiving the promises of God. You can spend a few minutes several times a day receiving the prayer promises of Jesus and the healing words of the Bible. Write down three or four Scripture verses and repeat them to yourself again and again. At first this may seem only an exercise of the mind, but at some point the truth of these words will begin to enter your heart. You will begin to believe them. They will become personal revelation from the Lord to you. In other words, you will know He is speaking to you. Faith will rise up within you, for faith is believing what God has already done for you in Christ. He bore your sicknesses and carried your diseases, and by His wounds you are healed.

When you come to the time of prayer, you will meet with God first in His forgiveness and be set free from your sin and the wrong attitudes toward others. But you will also come with faith in your heart because, by the activity of the Holy Spirit, you believe these words of promise in your heart.

When you are ministering to others, it is very seldom that you need to lay hands on them immediately unless it is a case of extremity. It is much better to prepare people properly and to ensure they are in a place of faith before praying with them. *People cannot have confidence about receiving from Jesus unless they know they are forgiven and are in an attitude of forgiveness toward others.* They also need to receive the healing promises of His Word into their hearts so that they know it is Jesus' purpose to give to them.

DIFFERENT MEANS

There are several ways in which God heals, but all are to be accompanied with faith in His love, mercy, and grace. Anointing or the laying on of hands is a point at which your faith can be released to God. There is nothing magical in the hands. I would certainly not allow anyone who claimed to have a gift of healing in the hands to lay hands on me. Christians will lay hands on people who are sick, and they will recover because of their faith in the atoning work of Jesus and the promises of His Word, not because someone has been endowed with magical powers. Many people who are involved in the occult claim such powers.

At the moment of receiving the laying on of hands or anointing, those present believe that God honors His Word, and the previously sick person receives His healing. Their prayer of agreement can be immensely powerful in its results. "If two of you on earth agree about anything you ask," Jesus said, "it will be done for you by my Father in heaven" (Matt. 18:19). Concerning *anything!* That includes healing.

When giving directions about anointing for people who are sick, James makes it clear that there is to be a mutual confession of sins. Those ministering need to ensure that there is no impediment to their being used by God as open channels of the Holy Spirit, that nothing can hinder their sensitivity to His voice and leading.

When you pray, speak to the mountain. You are coming against the work of the enemy, and you have authority to overcome all his powers. You are coming against the sickness God does not want. Do not doubt in your heart that the mountain will be moved.

PRAYER PATTERN

This then is the general pattern:

- Prepare by praising the Lord for His love, grace, and mercy.
- Come humbly to the Lord, confessing your sins.

- Make sure you are right with other people.
- Be conscious of the Lord's presence and His faithfulness to His words of promise. Your faith is in what He has both done and said.
- Speak to the mountain, commanding it to move in the name of Jesus.
- Through praying the prayer of faith, agreeing with others or using a sacramental act such as the laying on of hands or anointing, allow the power of the Holy Spirit to come upon you, and believe you are receiving God's answer to your need.
- End with a prayer of thanksgiving and praise to God. His Word says, "Everyone who asks receives" (Matt. 7:8). The prayer of faith is always prayed in a context of praise because of the heart knowledge of God's faithfulness. Praise focuses our attention on Him, and we realize what a great and mighty God He is, the merciful Lord who wants to heal. Hallelujah!

If you believe, you will receive whatever you ask for in prayer (Matt. 21:22).

23

FAITH AND HOPE

Many people become confused because they fail to distinguish properly between faith and hope. In Scripture, hope relates to what God *will do* in the future. We have a sure and certain Christian hope. For example, we hope that Jesus will

100 RECEIVING YOUR HEALING

come again not as the suffering Servant but as the triumphant King of glory. We firmly believe in this hope: "Now faith is being sure of what we hope for" (Heb. 11:1). But believing it now does not make it happen now. This is what God *will do* at His appointed hour. Believing today that Jesus will come again doesn't make Him come again today.

We also believe we will be raised from the dead and reign eternally with God in His glory because of what God has done for us in Jesus. We firmly believe that; it is part of our hope. It relates to the future, to what will happen after you die. It is not your expectation that you are going to drop down dead within the next few minutes so that a resurrection can take place! As a Christian, you can have assurance that when you die physically, you will go to be with the Lord; that is part of your hope.

HEALED BY FAITH, NOT HOPE

When ministering healing, Jesus does not talk in terms of hope, for healing is available to us now through the work of His cross. When He teaches about how to pray with faith, He says, "Whatever you ask for in prayer [that means, anytime you ask God for anything], believe that you have received it, and it will be yours" (Mark 11:24).

Hope is concerned with what God will do; faith is concerned with what He has done, with what He makes available to us now. When you pray with hope, you say He will do something in the future. When you pray with faith, you believe that you have received what you ask for. Then you are certain in your heart that it will be yours.

It is distressing to find many groups of people disheartened because they were praying for someone who was seriously ill but the person died instead of being healed. "We were so sure that God was going to heal her," they say. "We really believed she was going to be healed." Often they conclude, "Our faith has been shattered because she wasn't healed." Lovingly and gently they need to be shown that they were not in a place of faith. Faith doesn't say, "God will, at some time in the future." Faith says, "God *has.*" *Faith knows that the healing is accomplished.*

Jesus bore your sicknesses on the cross.
By His stripes you are healed.
Your faith enables you to receive the benefit of what He has done.
If He has done all that is necessary for your healing, do not give up.
Persist in faith.

[He] forgives all your sins and heals all your diseases (Ps. 103:3).

24

PERSISTENTLY THANKFUL

Jesus taught the parable about the persistent widow to show His disciples that "they should always pray and not give up" (Luke 18:1). She was not to be put off; she continued in her requests until she knew she had received the right answer. Jesus added, "And will not God bring about justice for his chosen ones, who cry out to him day and night? Will he keep putting them off? I tell you, he will see that they get justice, and quickly. However, when the Son of Man comes, will he find faith on the earth?" (Luke 18:7–8).

That is the crucial question!

PERSEVERANCE

Even when you have the witness of faith in your heart, you will still need to persevere in prayer. *But you will be persevering in prayer with thanksgiving*, and you know inevitably that your healing will be manifested; it is already yours—you have assurance of that.

James tells us, "Consider it pure joy, my brothers, whenever you face trials of many kinds, because you know that the testing of your faith develops perseverance. Perseverance must finish its work so that you may be mature and complete, not lacking anything" (James 1:2–4).

It is through such times of testing that God builds your trust and confidence in Him. Some people say that the real evidence of faith is demonstrated by instantaneous answers to prayer. We all enjoy those answers and wish they would happen on every occasion. But God strengthens your faith by taking you through times of waiting. Such times test the genuineness of your faith. How many times have you begun to believe God for something, but somewhere along the way you have given up trusting Him for the answer? The Lord knew from the beginning you did not truly believe Him, you had no true revelation of faith in your heart, and you were not prepared to inherit the promises by faith with patience (Heb. 11:39).

FAITH WITH THANKSGIVING

Some people suggest that once the prayer of faith has been prayed, there is no necessity to be concerned about that matter anymore; God has it in hand. This idea can lead to the notion that we should never pray for a need more than once.

But there are times when we need to persevere in prayer, perhaps until we come to a place of genuine faith.

We know it is possible to imagine we are full of faith for a particular situation. But if we do not receive an immediate answer, unbelief is easily exposed. God has been aware of the questions deep in our hearts, and His delay exposes those uncertainties to us.

When Jesus says, "Ask and you will receive," the word *ask* is in the continuous tense, meaning to go on asking, to continue to ask.

However, once you know you have received the answer, even if there is no immediate outward change, you need to persevere in prayer with thanksgiving. *You know you have received the answer, so continue to rejoice in the Lord for His goodness and faithfulness to His Word:* "Do not be anxious about anything, but in everything, by prayer and petition, *with thanksgiving*, present your requests to God. And the peace of God, which transcends all understanding, will guard your hearts and your minds in Christ Jesus" (Phil. 4:6–7, italics mine).

This word about peace is often quoted out of context. Paul says that God's peace, which is beyond our understanding, will descend on us when we pray and ask God *with thanksgiving*. In that simple act, we express faith in the Lord's faithfulness. There is no need to strive. We are able to persist in that thanksgiving with the utmost confidence that His promise—*it will be yours*—shall be fulfilled.

If that thanksgiving turns to pleading, it is an indication that faith was lacking in the first place. The people do not truly believe they *have* received.

Faith and thanksgiving belong together: "Be joyful always; pray continually; give thanks in all circumstances, for this is God's will for you in Christ Jesus" (1 Thess. 5:16–18). When Jesus prayed over the loaves and fish before feeding the multitude, He gave thanks to His Father. Before commanding Lazarus to come from the tomb, He prayed, "Father, I thank you that you have heard me" (John 11:41). At the Last Supper, He gave thanks over the bread and the cup before proclaiming them to be His body and blood.

Notice that Jesus gave thanks to God *before* the supernatural events took place. Paul says, "So then, just as you received Christ Jesus as Lord, continue to live in him, rooted and built up in him, *strengthened in the faith* as you were taught, and *overflowing with thankfulness*" (Col. 2:6–7, italics mine).

REJOICE ALWAYS

We are to "rejoice in the Lord always." This is the attitude God wants. If our thoughts are upon ourselves, our circumstances, or our fears, we certainly shall not be rejoicing. But if the Lord has His rightful place, we shall be people who praise; our minds are set upon things above, rejoicing in the Lord in the midst of every difficulty. *Faith is expressed in such rejoicing*, and so God's power is then released into the situation to free us from the difficulty. It is possible to resent having the problem, to be angry with God for allowing it, to be angry with others for causing it, to be angry with ourselves for receiving it, but *until we rejoice in the Lord, we are unlikely to see much of His power released into the situation.* Hear the words again:

Rejoice in the Lord always. I will say it again: Rejoice! Let your gentleness be evident to all. The Lord is near. Do not be anxious about anything, but in everything, by prayer and petition, with thanksgiving, present your requests to God. And the peace of God, which transcends all understanding, will guard your hearts and your minds in Christ Jesus (Phil. 4:4–7).

You need a mind that is kept or guarded in Christ, not full of fear and sickness but full of peace because you trust the Lord.

CONFLICT AND VICTORY

The commission Jesus gives to His church is to heal people who are sick, not simply to pray prayers for them or over them. That commission can be fulfilled only if we have an expectation of success. Jesus has not called and commissioned us to failure. We can cry with Paul, "But thanks be to God! He gives us the victory through our Lord Jesus Christ" (1 Cor. 15:57).

Sometimes people come to me and say, "Will you pray a little prayer for me?" My answer is, "No, I will pray a big prayer for you." It doesn't have to be a long prayer, but it has to be an expectant prayer so that as we come against sickness, we have the victory in Jesus' name.

The enemy does not want to remove sickness; it is possible, therefore, to experience a genuine conflict over a period of time as the power of God comes against the disease and drives it from the body. There are miracles when healing happens in an instant; but there are many occasions when the healing takes place over a period of time as the person continues to stand on God's Word with faith and thanksgiving.

It need not bother you if, during that time, you receive the laying on of hands on a number of occasions, so long as you are continuing to proclaim the victory of Jesus that is already taking place. You are praying by faith with thanksgiving. You are coming against that disease in His name; you are driving it out with His power.

There will be much battling of the wrong kind if you do not believe you have the victory. Just as it is impossible to be in faith unless you *know* it is God's will to heal you, so it is unlikely you will see much happen in praying for yourself or others unless you know you have the victory in Jesus' name *before* you pray. You are able to give thanks *before* the event as if it had already happened. That is the way Jesus prayed, and if you pray in His name, on His behalf, and with His authority, that is the way you are able to pray.

When you are in faith before you ask, you expect results and look for them. Unbelief says that you could not truly expect it to happen; it would be too much to hope for. Faith believes you have the answer.

Your faith is not in the improvement or lack of immediate change; you faith is in the Lord and His Word, knowing that it will be yours.

Rejoice in the Lord always.
Pray with thanksgiving.
Persevere in thankfulness.
Always expect God to answer with His power.

Do not be anxious about anything, but in everything, by prayer and petition, with thanksgiving, present your requests to God (Phil. 4:6).

25

GIVE AND YOU
WILL RECEIVE

One of the spiritual principles Jesus teaches is summed up in this statement: "The measure you give is the measure you get back." If you want to receive from God, you need to take seriously what the Scriptures say about giving.

GOD OF GRACE

God is the God of grace; He gives freely to those who deserve nothing. You can never deserve to receive from Him. He gives because He loves you. He gives because He chooses to give to you. He gives because He has promised to give to you. He gives because His Son gave His life for you. He gives because He is merciful and gracious.

He has made you in His own image. He wants you to be like Him. Because He loves, He wants you to love. Because He is the God of grace, He wants you to be gracious. Because He is generous, He wants you to be generous. Your willingness to give enables you to receive freely from the Lord. If you are ever short on receiving what you need from Him, consider what you are giving to Him.

KINGDOM PRINCIPLE

This is a spiritual principle of God's kingdom evident in many areas of Jesus' teaching. He said,

> Give, and it will be given to you. A good measure, pressed down, shaken together and running over, will be poured into your lap. For with the measure you use, it will be measured to you (Luke 6:38).

This principle is worked out in many different ways, both positive and negative. For example, it is true of judgment and condemnation:

> Do not judge, and you will not be judged. Do not condemn, and you will not be condemned (Luke 6:37).

It is true of showing mercy to others:

> Blessed are the merciful, for they will be shown mercy (Matt. 5:7).

It is true of forgiveness:

> Forgive us our debts, as we also have forgiven our debtors (Matt. 6:12).

> For if you forgive men when they sin against you, your heavenly Father will also forgive you. But if you do not forgive men their sins, your Father will not forgive your sins (Matt. 6:14–15).

> Forgive, and you will be forgiven (Luke 6:37).

> And when you stand praying, if you hold anything against anyone, forgive him, so that your Father in heaven may forgive you your sins (Mark 11:25).

The same principle applies to financial giving:

> Remember this: Whoever sows sparingly will also reap
> sparingly, and whoever sows generously will also reap
> generously. Each man should give what he has decided in
> his heart to give, not reluctantly or under compulsion, for
> God loves a cheerful giver (2 Cor. 9:6–7).

The principle is clear: if you give little, you receive little;
if you give much, you receive much. It is not the amount that
matters but the degree of sacrifice, love, faith, and obedience
involved in the giving. This is not to imply that it is possible
to buy blessing from God. Paul knows well that everything we
receive comes as an expression of the Lord's grace. But he
makes clear what the consequences of faithful and joyful
giving are in the very next verse: "And God is able to make
all grace abound to you, so that in all things at all times,
having all that you need, you will abound in every good work"
(2 Cor. 9:8).

How wise God is! He knows we cannot give to others what
we have not first received ourselves. The more of His riches
that are poured into our lives, the more we have to give to
others. There is an endless circle of giving. You give to the
Lord; He gives His good measure back to you. You then have
even more to give, and He then pours greater abundance into
your life. You give more again, and He gives still more back
to you: "Now he who supplies seed to the sower and bread for
food will also supply and increase your store of seed and will
enlarge the harvest of your righteousness" (v. 10). And what
is the outcome? "You will be made rich in every way so that
you can be generous on every occasion, and through us your
generosity will result in thanksgiving to God" (v. 11).

GIVING ENABLES RECEIVING

The act of giving opens our hearts to God and enables us to receive the healing and material blessings He wants to pour into our lives.

In Malachi, God says we can test His faithfulness in honoring the faithful giving of money by His people. He tells the people to bring the whole tithe, the *first* tenth of *all* they earn or receive, "and see if I will not throw open the floodgates of heaven and pour out so much blessing that you will not have room enough for it" (Mal. 3:10).

Some argue that tithing is not specifically taught in the New Testament and is not, therefore, necessary for Christians, who are to live by grace, not law. Such a position shows misunderstanding of the Scriptures. The Christian gives not because of legal duty but because of a heart of generous love. In the New Testament, not only the first tenth belongs to the Lord, but *everything* belongs to Him. Because we have been purchased by the blood of Jesus that we may belong to the Father, everything we are and have is the Lord's. He expects more, not less, for His new covenant children. And the promises of blessing He gives are likewise greater.

So the Christian demonstrates love for the Lord by giving *at least* the first tenth of his total income—and more! This is seed that when planted will produce a harvest many times the amount of seed sown. The proverb states,

> One man gives freely, yet gains even more;
> another withholds unduly, but comes to poverty.
> A generous man will prosper (11:24–25).

The Christian needs to take care *where* she gives. There is little point in sowing seed in lifeless desert soil. She gives to the King for the work of the kingdom, knowing that if she seeks first the kingdom and God's righteousness, He will meet every need, according to the promise of His Word: "And God is able to make *all* grace abound to *you*, so that in *all* things at *all* times, having *all* that you need, you will abound in every good work" (2 Cor. 9:8, italics mine).

This is the spiritual principle: if you are to receive from the Lord, then first give to Him. You can give only because God has first given to you. You can love only because He has first loved you.

God had to work according to His own principles. Before He could receive many children into His kingdom, He first had to give His own Son as a sacrifice for sin. When Jesus went to the cross, He paid the price for you so that you might belong to His kingdom and receive all its benefits. Everything you are and all you have is the Lord's. You do not own any part of your life. Either you are His, or you do not belong to Him. It is a question of all or nothing.

It is meaningless to say, "Part of me belongs to God, and part belongs to myself. Part of my money and possessions belongs to Him, and part belongs to me." No, everything is His. If I love the Lord, I want to reflect His generosity: "For you know the grace of our Lord Jesus Christ, that though he was rich, yet for your sakes he became poor, so that you through his poverty might become rich" (2 Cor. 8:9).

Jesus became a curse to free you from the curse of poverty, the curse of sickness, the curse of sin, the curse of Satan's dominion over you.

WITH FAITH, LOVE, AND JOY

Faith is expressed by your willingness to give and trust God to honor His Word to measure back to you in the way He promises. The world says that if you give, you will have less and be worse off. Jesus tells us the principle of His kingdom is the opposite. If you give, you will have more and will be better off.

Remember, *you cannot buy blessing, and giving does not produce faith for healing. It is an expression of love and faith already in the heart and opens the way to receive from God the abundance of the riches He desires to give.*

Jesus taught, "It is more blessed to give than to receive" (Acts 20:35).

Many have discovered the joy of praying for other sick people when they have a healing need themselves. This prayer not only is an expression of a kingdom principle but also avoids an excess of self-concern and enables the person to concentrate on the Lord as healer. This act of praying for others to be healed is an expression of love for them, not simply a device to receive healing yourself!

When you give, do so out of the sheer joy of giving. When you give to someone in obedience to Him, you experience a bubble of joy inside because you have done something that God wants. You have fulfilled His desire for you, and you have expressed something of the love, graciousness, and generosity of Jesus. That is why giving makes you feel good, peaceful, and contented. By being faithful to God in your giving, you can always expect He will be faithful in His giving to you.

He is the God of grace, and He is able to make His grace, His giving, abound to you so that in *all* things at *all* times, you might have *all* you need. Don't alter the Word of God; believe what He says. It is God's purpose to give to you on all occasions everything that you need, and that includes your healing. *Giving releases God's giving into your life.*

God is willing to give His healing to you so that you can learn to give His healing to others. Many people who have been healed by the Lord then have faith to believe that God can use them to minister His healing to others. God does not act for our selfish indulgence. He heals for His own glory because He loves to heal and to meet the needs of His children. And He heals to make us more effective witnesses of His grace and goodness.

Of course there is always an element of self-desire when asking God to heal; it would be foolish not to acknowledge that. But God wants us to have a motive beyond that. We are not taking from Him only for ourselves; we approach Him with a desire to give ourselves to Him. We want to be healed so that we can offer Him not a sick life but a healed one that He might use us for His praise and His glory.

> *The measure you give will be the measure you receive.*
> *God's kingdom principle applies to you.*
> *Do not withhold from God what is rightfully His.*
> *Give, and expect Him to give His good measure back to you.*
> *As you are faithful in giving to God, so He will prove Himself faithful in giving to you.*

Give, and it will be given to you. A good measure, pressed down, shaken together and running over, will be poured into your lap. For with the measure you use, it will be measured to you (Luke 6:38).

26

OBEY

Jesus came to Peter's house where his mother-in-law was lying in bed with a fever. Jesus "touched her hand and the fever left her, and she got up and began to wait on him" (Matt. 8:15). That is a good motive for seeking God's healing in your life—so that you may rise up and serve Him.

There is little point in saying, "Lord, please heal me so that I can go on being disobedient to You." Although God never wills sickness on us, He can use it positively to bring us to obedience. Pain and sickness can cause you to reassess what you are doing with your life. God would much prefer you to be attentive to His voice and willing to obey Him while in good health, without waiting until you are ill before listening to Him. When you are ill, you have to listen!

There is no lesson God teaches us in sickness that He would not prefer to teach us in health!

If you believe that God has allowed sickness in your life to teach you some lesson, you had better ask Him to make clear what He is saying and respond quickly. Logically, He will make sure that the sickness is removed as soon as you have obeyed what He is saying. There would be no purpose in allowing the illness to persist beyond the point of usefulness.

CONFIDENCE FROM OBEDIENCE

God's promises of answered prayer need to be seen in context. He does not promise us healing unconditionally, regardless of our conduct. Obedience and faith go together in the Scriptures.

We cannot expect the Holy Spirit to bring us to confidence of faith in a particular situation if we are being deliberately disobedient to the Lord in some way. The disciple John heard Jesus give all His wonderful prayer promises. About fifty years later, after all those years of experience of Spirit-filled ministry, he wrote, "Dear friends, if our hearts do not condemn us, we have confidence before God and receive from him anything we ask, because we obey his commands and do what pleases him" (1 John 3:21–22).

John says clearly that God does fulfill Jesus' promise to give us whatever we ask in His name when these three conditions are fulfilled:

1. *Our hearts do not condemn us.* There is no unconfessed sin, the guilt of which could steal our confidence before God.

2. *We obey His commands.* Many of His promises are linked to His words of positive direction for our lives.

3. *We do what pleases Him.* To agree with His words and to live them put us in a good position to have faith that He will answer our needs.

We cannot expect to be in a position to receive healing if we are rejecting His Word for other areas of our lives. *Often the Lord will wait until an issue of obedience to Him is settled before He will allow the healing to take place.*

John goes on to point out, "And this is his command: to believe in the name of his Son, Jesus Christ, and to love one another as he commanded us. Those who obey his commands live in him, and he in them" (1 John 3:23–24)

BE CAREFUL

We must be very careful that we do not slip into the idea that God wants us to be sick or that He sends sickness as a punishment. Satan is the perpetrator of sickness, and we are to resist him. Often there is no other motive behind the sickness than the enemy's desire to steal, kill, and destroy. He loves to hinder God's children in any way possible.

Disobedience to the Lord gives the enemy the opportunity to afflict us in various ways. It is not that God decides to inflict sickness on us; it is simply that persistent disobedience will have serious consequences for us, and one of those possible consequences is illness. *Disobedience makes us vulnerable.*

We must also remember that nowhere do the Gospels record Jesus as even suggesting to any of the multitudes coming to Him for healing that their sickness was given to them to teach them a lesson. It would be incongruous for the Father to inflict a child with sickness to discipline her and for the Son to remove the Father's handiwork. That is not the way He operates. God is not divided against Himself.

Does Jesus say to anyone, "Go away. I will not heal you. This sickness is sent to teach you a lesson"? No. He heals all who come to Him. But He does warn people to turn away from their sins lest worse things happen to them.

The disciples asked Jesus, "Rabbi, who sinned, this man or his parents, that he was born blind?" Jesus answered, "Neither this man nor his parents sinned, but this happened so that the work of God might be displayed in his life" (John 9:2–3).

The work of God is to believe in the One He sent. Faith in Jesus brings the healing that gives glory to God.

If ever you are sick, you can know the redeeming love of Jesus. Sickness and pain cause us to open our hearts to Him to see if any repentance is needed. The existence of the need makes us more responsive to Him. He can use the situation creatively, but that does not mean He wants the need to persist.

You hear of people who thank God for their illnesses and problems because they help to keep them close to the Lord. They lose some of their fleshly desires during sickness, and so they receive the illness as a way of controlling the flesh.

This is a travesty of God's purpose. He teaches us in His Word that we are to walk in the Spirit, not the flesh, and He shows us how we are to reckon ourselves dead to the old life and no longer under control of the flesh. Nowhere does He suggest that sickness is given to control the flesh. He wants us walking in health, fulfilling His kingdom purposes, not languishing in our beds, thankful that we are not so prone to certain areas of temptation. To yield to sickness in that way is in itself a work of the flesh.

RESPONSIVE TO THE LORD

An anointed man of God with a national ministry was laid flat on his back for five months with a spinal problem. During that time, he met with the Lord in a truly significant way that transformed his ministry. It would be tempting to suggest that the illness was God's purpose. But the Lord made clear to him that He had been trying to get his attention over certain matters for some time, but the man would not be still enough to listen. The illness gave him the opportunity to hear what he had refused to hear earlier. God used the sickness creatively but would have preferred His servant to respond long before. It took five months for him to face what the Lord was saying. When he did, his healing began immediately.

Many think they are too busy to wait on the Lord or to listen to what He is saying. Others ignore the warnings God gives them as they abuse their bodies in overindulgence or overactivity. Some fail to take notice of the fact that they need physical exercise and recreation. Bodies that are not treated properly cry out in protest sooner or later. Then people are more prepared to take notice of the voice of God that has been drowned by the clamor of their business and self-concern.

God wants to heal you that you might serve Him and be obedient to the leading of the Spirit in your life. His best purposes will not be served by leaving you in sickness.

If you think God is teaching you something through an infirmity, learn the lesson quickly and be healed. Hear what He is saying and respond. That will remove any impediment to your healing. If God wants to teach you something, He will not make it difficult for you to understand what He is saying.

If you believe your healing is being hindered because of disobedience, come to Jesus with repentance, and bring your life back into line with His will and purpose. God has not imposed sickness on you to punish you. He imposed your sickness on Jesus when He went to the cross so that you might be set free from it. He wants you to be healed and serve Him.

> *God wants to be glorified in your life.*
> *It is not His purpose for you to accept sickness as His will for you.*
> *He will be glorified in your obedience to His Word.*
> *He will be glorified in your obedience to the heeding of the Holy Spirit.*
> *If you are too busy to hear the Lord, change your priorities immediately.*
> *Do not push away what He is saying to you. Respond with love, faith, and obedience.*

Call upon me in the day of trouble; I will deliver you, and you will honor me (Ps. 50:15).

27

THE BODY

There is a temptation among Christians to believe that because God is primarily concerned with the heart, He is not interested in their bodies. Nothing could be further from the truth. Jesus would not have spent so much time healing people physically if God was not concerned about their bodies.

There is ample evidence in Scripture that God has a vital role for the body. He has created you with a body to house your spirit and soul. God Himself came and lived in a human, physical body in the person of Jesus. As God expressed Himself in the physical body of His Son, so He wants to express Himself in you. Your body manifests what is happening in your soul and spirit. Because Jesus lives in you by the power of the Holy Spirit, He can express His life through your physical body.

He has not created you as a disembodied soul floating around in space. You need your body to express your personality. As a Christian, you need your body to express the life of Jesus in you.

NOT FOR IMMORALITY

The wicked will not inherit the kingdom of God. Sexual immorality and misuse of the body are widespread among unbelievers before their conversion. To Christians, Paul writes, "But you were washed, you were sanctified, you were justified in the name of the Lord Jesus Christ and by the Spirit of our God" (1 Cor. 6:11).

Having been made acceptable to God and having been brought into the glorious liberty of the children of God do not mean believers are free to do as they please with their bodies. Some had the attitude that everything was permissible for them. But Paul points out that not everything is beneficial, nor is it right to be mastered by anything. Not all the ways in which Christians use their bodies are beneficial to their spiritual welfare, let alone their physical well-being. It is never right for a Christian to be mastered by the body.

Paul says,

Therefore do not let sin reign in your mortal body so that you obey its evil desires. Do not offer the parts of your body to sin, as instruments of wickedness, but rather offer yourselves to God, as those who have been brought from death to life; and offer the parts of your body to him as instruments of righteousness (Rom. 6:12–13).

FOR THE LORD

"The body is not meant for sexual immorality, but for the Lord, and the Lord for the body" (1 Cor. 6:13). This is a key Scripture verse to understand. The body is for the Lord. He has given you a body not only to house your human spirit and soul but also to be a temple of the Holy Spirit. He wants the Spirit to be expressed through your physical body, flowing out of you as rivers of living water. *Your body is not for yourself; it is for the Lord. It is not for sickness; it is for the Lord.* God has not created your body to be sick; He does not desire it to be sick. This truth can give you further encouragement to turn to Him and expect Him to heal you whenever you are physically ill.

Not only is the body for the Lord, but also *the Lord is for the body*. He has come to live in you by the power of the Holy Spirit, and He wants the Spirit to be working for your physical well-being. Your body is a member of Christ Himself; this makes it very important to God. He has made you spiritually a member of a spiritual body, and your physical body is incorporated into Christ. That is why members of His body should not be united to a prostitute, and Christians should be very careful about the way in which they use the body: "Do you not know that your body is a temple of the Holy Spirit, who is in you, whom you have received from God? You are not your own; you were bought at a price. Therefore honor God with your body" (1 Cor. 6:19–20).

When Jesus died on the cross, He paid the price not only for your spirit, which will eventually go to heaven and live in glory with Him, but also for your body, which houses the Holy Spirit during your earthly existence. How important it is, therefore, to honor God with your body. He does not want you contracting sickness because of any misuse or abuse of your body. Your body belongs to the Lord and is to be treated accordingly.

TREAT YOUR BODY WITH RESPECT

God does not call us to foolishness. He has created us with certain physical limitations, and if we abuse our bodies, they are going to scream in protest. The devil wants people to be so busy that they abuse the physical bodies God has given them and then begin to suffer as a result. This does not mean we should be full of self-concern. Jesus said, "If anyone would come after me, he must deny himself and take up his cross and follow me" (Matt. 16:24).

Paul suffered much physical abuse for preaching the gospel—imprisonment, floggings, shipwreck, stoning—and was in constant danger of death. In addition, Paul wrote, "I have labored and toiled and have often gone without sleep; I have known hunger and thirst and have often gone without food; I have been cold and naked" (2 Cor. 11:27). More than anyone, he knew the cost of proclaiming the gospel.

Yet this does not give to any Christian the right to abuse the body deliberately, to neglect the need for rest and proper nourishment. Satan wants to inflict sickness upon people, and there is no need to assist him!

Jesus calls us to care in a right and proper way for our bodies and not to abuse them. For example, we are not to use them in a wrong way sexually or through greed. We are not to be lazy and self-indulgent. The damage done through smoking, excessive drinking, and illicit drug taking is well known. If we acknowledge that our bodies are temples of the Holy Spirit, God living in us, we will not abuse them in such ways.

There have been a number of occasions when God has given me a word for people about their weight. They are either overweight or seriously underweight and have often neglected the warnings given them by their doctors. If physical symptoms are the result of overweight, there is no point in coming to the Lord wanting to receive healing without losing weight. That is part of the very healing that God wants to bring into that person's life.

I prayed with an overweight woman with a serious knee complaint. God wonderfully healed her, and she went on her way rejoicing. A few months later she returned, concerned that her knee was beginning to cause her trouble again. "Have you seen your doctor?" I asked her. She had, and he had told her to lose weight. "That is also God's word to you," I said. When she obeyed, she had no further trouble with her knee.

The believer is able to do the will of God through the power of the Holy Spirit living in him; but he soon learns that his body often desires to do things that are alien to God's purposes. The body seeks attention, perhaps to be overfed or underfed to appear fashionable. The body desires sexual satisfaction, and many Christians experience great conflict in the area of sexual desire.

Christians no longer have to be ruled by their bodies' appetites. They will continue to experience conflict but are able to be victorious in it as they learn to trust in the Holy Spirit and not yield to the temptations of the flesh. They contain the riches of the Lord in earthen vessels and are very aware of physical weakness. *It is God's purpose to see the Holy Spirit's power released in your life so that your body receives life and health from His indwelling presence.* Then "he who raised Christ from the dead will also give life to your mortal bodies through his Spirit, who lives in you" (Rom. 8:11).

Your obligation is not to the sinful nature, to be ruled by its passions, but to the Holy Spirit.

In simple terms, you are not to allow your bodily appetites to rule you. *You are to live and walk in the Spirit and experience the Spirit giving life to your mortal body,* the body that you have during this life. It is God's purpose to give you life, to strengthen you physically, and to heal you when you are sick.

BODIES YIELDED TO THE LORD

Some people find it difficult to receive physical healing because they have not truly given their bodies to the Lord. Paul says, "Therefore, I urge you, brothers, in view of God's mercy, to offer your bodies as living sacrifices, holy and pleasing to God—this is your spiritual act of worship" (Rom. 12:1). This is the worship God desires: to see His children offering their bodies as living sacrifices, holy and pleasing to Him. Your body can be made holy only when offered to Him, consecrated to His purposes.

Many people have found great value in offering each part of their bodies in a very direct and positive way to the Lord. They give their eyes to see as Jesus would see and not to dwell on ungodly things. They give their ears to Him that they may be open to hear His Word rather than the gossip and opinions of men and women. They want to hear what is good, upbuilding, and positive. They give their mouths to the Lord to speak words that are wholesome and express faith rather than to speak unbelief, criticism, judgment, and other negative things. And so on, they yield every bodily function to be consecrated to the Lord.

If Christians lived continually with such consecration, they would not be so prone to sickness, and they would not experience so much stress, either emotionally or physically.

When we are sick, it is important to offer the body to the Lord to be healed. He can touch and heal only what is given and yielded to Him. There is little purpose in saying, "Lord, heal me," if you don't submit your body to Him to be healed.

THE BODY WEARS OUT

We have to distinguish healing needs from the natural aging processes to which our bodies are subject. When young, I suffered from double vision and had to wear glasses. The Lord healed that problem, and for eleven years, I was free from the need of glasses. Then with the amount of reading and writing I was doing in my present ministry, my eyes began to become tired.

When I prayed, I sensed the Lord was telling me to have my eyes tested. If I were to wear glasses, I would be able to see clearly and without strain. The thought caused me problems at first because I believed in healing and thought it would not be a good witness to be praying for others when I had an obvious need myself.

When my eyes were tested, the doctor suggested that I must have had surgery for my previous eye problem to have been corrected. My cure was from the heavenly surgeon! He then explained to me that my present problem was of a different order and was due to the natural aging process.

In such circumstances, the need to wear glasses is as natural as a man going bald or wrinkles appearing on aging skin. That does not mean that God cannot strengthen my eyes or that I am resigned to always having to wear glasses. It may be inconvenient to wear them, but the fact that I have to do so in no way impairs my life or work. Far from it; they are a considerable help.

It would be difficult if eye disease was seriously impairing my life. Then I would definitely need healing from the Lord.

I believe He has also made it clear that I should not be self-conscious in ministering His healing power to others while I have such an obvious weakness. This demonstrates two things: God is willing to work through weak, imperfect individuals, and doing so ensures the glory is given to Him for the healings that take place.

Maybe some will think that I am trying to accommodate the fact that I wear glasses. I trust not. I seek to be truthful with myself before the Lord.

The aging process leads to the inevitable death of the physical body, and this raises the question whether it is always right to pray for healing of older people.

Because people are advanced in age does not mean they have to resign themselves to painful sickness. As we grow older, we cannot do things we could do with ease when young. But many older people are healed of diseases, even though they may die naturally soon afterward. There is a difference between growing old and having disease invade the body.

I find it wise to pray for healing for an older or extremely sick person unless I have a clear sense from God that the person is going to die, in which case I need to prepare her for this great event. It is difficult not to be jealous of those who are going to be with the Lord!

> *Have you ever offered your body in detail to the Lord?*
> *Have you ever given your body not only to be a temple of*
>   *the Holy Spirit but also to walk in obedience to Him?*
> *If not, then you need to do that immediately.*
> *Do not allow a failure to present your body to the Lord to*
>   *hinder you from receiving healing from Him.*

The body is not meant for sexual immorality, but for the Lord, and the Lord for the body (1 Cor. 6:13).

||||||||||||||||||||||||||||||||||||||||||||||||||||||||

Part Five

HEALING OF MIND
AND EMOTIONS

||||||||||||||||||||||||||||||||||||||||||||||||||||||||

28

RENEW YOUR THINKING

Before you were born again and became a Christian, you belonged to the dominion of Satan, the kingdom of darkness. His spiritual kingdom is utterly negative because he is a thief, the father of lies, the deceiver of God's people, who loves to steal, kill, and destroy. He is the god of this age who blinds the minds of unbelievers.

When you gave your life to Jesus and He became your Savior and Lord, God rescued you from the dominion of darkness and brought you into the kingdom of the Son He loves (Col. 1:13). God began then to work a great transformation in your mind.

Repentance, turning to God, involves a change of mind, a change in your whole thinking about God, about yourself, and about His purpose for you. Before your conversion, Satan had free access to your mind, and he was able to feed in all kinds of negative thoughts. In many ways you became conditioned to looking at circumstances from a natural or worldly viewpoint. When you became a Christian, the light of Jesus began to shine into the spiritual darkness of your mind.

RESIST THOUGHTS OF SICKNESS

Because Satan has blinded the minds of unbelievers, they are unable to understand Jesus or the things of the Spirit. The Scriptures seem lifeless instead of being to them the Word of

God. They are unable to perceive spiritual truth because of their blindness; they are without revelation in their hearts. But when a person turns to Christ, He begins to shine His light into that darkness.

Satan, however, does not want to yield territory that has been his own, and so he still tries to influence your mind. He can sow a thought about physical sickness. It may come almost unnoticed, a suggestion that you may die of cancer or catch the flu. He does not announce himself by saying that Satan is about to speak to you. Deception is his business. The thought may be brief, but it needs to be resisted immediately in the name of Jesus.

You can either receive the negative thought or reject it. Many receive it, and it thus becomes a part of their thinking: *I might have cancer. I am bound to catch the flu. I shall always have a weak stomach.* If you receive the first negative thought, Satan will continue to feed you with further negative thoughts. If you believe the first, you are likely to believe the second and the third and each subsequent one.

He will reinforce his suggestions with subtle arguments: *There is cancer in your family. This disease is hereditary; you are bound to show the symptoms of it sooner or later. Look what happened to your friend; you are next.*

His greatest deception is to encourage you to think that such thoughts come from yourself, that they are part of you and you must accept them as inevitable. If you do not recognize their real source, you will not rebuke them, refuse to accept them, and dismiss them.

He can also sound very rational and reasonable. He will try to distract you from believing Scripture, for he knows these are words of spirit, life, and health. He will often point out to you the experience of others. "If so-and-so was not healed, why should you be? He was a man with much greater faith than you have." Subtle, because what he suggests seems so reasonable and right—but isn't: he is the deceiver.

When you listen to the enemy, fear lurks beneath the surface of your mind. When you listen to God's words of truth, you are liberated from such fear.

Learn to resist immediately every attempt of Satan to sow any negative thoughts in your mind. The enemy often tries such things with me, especially when I am ministering to other people who are sick. He suggests, "You could get that." I not only reject the thought in the name of Jesus but also declare the positive truth: "I'm not going to have that disease. God has created me not to be sick but to be whole and healthy, and He does not want me or any of His children to live in constant fear of sickness."

FEAR NOT

Fear of cancer is very common. Sometimes when doctors diagnose cancer, you hear people say, "I dreaded this," or "I always knew I would get it." Their negative faith has been tragically fulfilled. Others say to the doctor, "It's cancer, isn't it, doctor?" even though there may be no grounds for their fears. So deep can be their dread that they refuse to believe the doctor, even when the doctor genuinely assures them that there is no need for such fears.

Your mind is to be renewed so that you know the good, perfect, and acceptable will of God (Rom. 12:2). His will for you is *not* sickness. God is not glorified in the works of Satan. He can redeem the sickness, but He is not going to be glorified in it; He is glorified in healing. He is glorified in what He can do in the lives of people to enable them to overcome difficulty, but God cannot be glorified in sickness itself; He regards it as a curse.

God wants you to understand and appreciate this, for *the battle for health begins in your mind.* He wants you to be full of peace, trust, and confidence, not tension, fear, or conflict. He is ready to give you the peace that passes all understanding.

To allow your mind to dwell on the negative is destructive of faith and will quickly quench the work of the Spirit. God will speak positively to you, so do not listen instead to the enemy's negative lies and suggestions.

Is there an area in your thinking where Jesus is still not reigning? Is there an area of fear of sickness or disease, of the future, of the dark, of open spaces, or of being enclosed? Jesus is able to free you from all these things. He hasn't created you to be a person of fear: "Perfect love drives out fear" (1 John 4:18).

Paul helps Timothy to counteract the fears he experienced by directing him to the truth: "For God did not give us a spirit of timidity, but a spirit of power, of love and of self-discipline" (2 Tim. 1:7). God has put the same Holy Spirit in you; He is a spirit not of fear but of faith and boldness. The thief, Satan, likes to steal your peace by encouraging fear. There is a good acrostic for fear: *F*alse *E*xpectations *A*ppearing *R*eal. God wants you to have faith expectations. Fear can produce negative results; *faith will produce positive ones.* When you receive fears, they become part of you. It is difficult to trust God because you are more likely to listen to your fears. *Stand against the fears in the name of Jesus.* Do not let them become part of you.

Those who believe partially in God's love for them are delivered from some of their fears; those who know the perfection of His love are freed from all of them. Trust in yourself, believe your feelings and circumstances, and you are likely to fear; *trust in the Lord's unfailing love for you, and you will walk in faith, not fear.*

When the enemy shoots at you, take the shield of faith

against all those thoughts and fears. With that shield you are able to quench all the fiery darts of the evil one. Hallelujah!

> *Do not allow your thoughts to dwell on yourself, your fears, and your failures.*
> *Resist every attempt by the enemy to sow seeds of sickness in your mind.*
> *Fill your mind with the positive truth of God's Word.*

His faithfulness will be your shield and rampart.
You will not fear the terror of night,
   nor the arrow that flies by day,
nor the pestilence that stalks in the darkness,
   nor the plague that destroys at midday (Ps. 91:4–6).

29

A RENEWED MIND

We have divine power to demolish the strongholds of the enemy. We are able to "take captive every thought to make it obedient to Christ" (2 Cor. 10:5). *We do not have to allow the enemy to influence our minds, and we certainly do not have to let him control any area of our thinking.*

EVIL THOUGHTS

Do you have lustful or greedy thoughts? Do not be surprised that the enemy fires such things at you. It is not a sin to be tempted, but what you do with the temptation is of prime importance. The sin is yielding to the temptation. Rebuke and reject the lustful and greedy thoughts just as you would the thoughts of sickness, pain, and disease.

If you love the Lord, you certainly don't want unholy and ungodly thoughts in your mind. Where do they come from? The enemy! At any moment of holiness, he wants to attack you with his unholiness, to try to feed into your mind whatever is opposed to God's purposes.

Satan loves to try to destroy your concentration or sow confusion in your mind, especially when you are praying. The enemy will do anything to distract you then, for he understands the power of prayer.

There is no point in becoming anxious or imagining you cannot pray. You need to appreciate what is happening and put the enemy in his place. Say, "Satan, you have no business here and no right to distract me. Go in the name of Jesus." *If you resist the devil, he will flee from you, for He who is in you, the Holy Spirit, is greater than he that is in the world, Satan.*

It is not only thoughts of sickness that are negative and destructive of faith. Critical, lying, jealous, unforgiving, and judgmental thoughts equally need to be resisted. These can result from wrong heart attitudes toward others, but they can also be encouraged by suggestions from the enemy. Your mind is not his territory but is to be set on things above.

Satan will also be quick to point out your failures and try to make you feel condemned for them. Your mind needs not only to be cleansed of negative thoughts but to be filled with positive ones.

The enemy will also try to sow seeds of doubt concerning your healing, pointing you to the circumstances, feelings, or symptoms—anything to distract you from believing God's Word. Even when you have received personal revelation by the Spirit, he will contradict what you have heard or suggest that you must be mistaken, that it could not have been a true word from God.

Understand that Satan is your enemy as he is God's enemy. But remember you have victory over him because Jesus has already defeated him.

AGAINST PREJUDICE AND TRADITION

Is there an area of your thinking where Jesus is not reigning? Is there an area of prejudice, even religious prejudice, because of what you have been taught or because of your own opinions? Are you bound more to the traditions of the church than to a love for Jesus and faith in His Word? Human-devised traditions nullify the Word of God and so make it impossible to express faith. Jesus said, "Thus you nullify the Word of God by your tradition that you have handed down. And you do many things like that" (Mark 7:13). Let the Holy Spirit show you where you need to come against those areas of wrong thinking so that the truth of God's Word may be established in your mind and your attitudes may be changed.

The unbelief and doubts that Satan wants to sow in your mind undermine the work of healing, of being able to receive and exercise faith in the way that is necessary. Satan knows that if he can influence your thinking, he will influence your believing. If he can prevent you from being positive in your mind, he will prevent you from being positive in your faith.

THINK GOD'S THOUGHTS

"Set your mind on things above, not on earthly things," Paul says (Col. 3:2). Fill your mind with the positive so that there is little room for the negative: "Finally, brothers, whatever is true, whatever is noble, whatever is right, whatever is pure, whatever is lovely, whatever is admirable—if anything is excellent or praiseworthy—think about such things" (Phil. 4:8).

Not only is it important to resist the negative influences that attack your mind, but also your thinking needs to be full of the positive words of God concerning your health and well-being: "Dear friend, I pray that you may enjoy good health and that all may go well with you, even as your soul is getting along well" (3 John 2).

A renewed mind thinks with God's thoughts. The believer fills the mind with His positive words. If you resist only the negative, your mind is left in a neutral state, waiting for the next attack. It is better to fill it with God's thoughts. Then not only is it easier to resist the negative but also His positive words create life and health in you.

It is important not only to read the Bible and meditate on it but also to receive into your heart the truths it contains. When you read a verse you know is particularly relevant to you, repeat it to yourself many times; let it become part of your thinking. Store up His promises within you. The Holy Spirit will take from this deposit of truth and speak positively to you, the right word at the right time.

PREVENTIVE MEDICINE

God wants you to live in expectation of health and strength, not physical sickness and disease. He does not want you to wait until you are sick and then ask Him to free you of the difficulty. He believes in preventive spiritual medicine; He would prefer to teach you to live in health. That begins in your mind, by having the right mental attitudes. This is a question not of mind over matter but of the Spirit working in your mind and through your body because you believe the truth.

Mind over matter is in part successful, but Christians have a much greater advantage over others because they know God's words are truth, spirit, life, and healing within them. When those words are stored in their hearts, they become a wellspring of life.

It is not enough to know Scripture verses; feed on them. *Feed on the words of Jesus, for He is the bread of life.* Allow your thinking to come more and more in line with God's thinking—about you, about His purposes for you, and about your health and well-being.

> *Resist the devil's thoughts with God's words.*
> *Bring your thinking in line with God's thoughts.*
> *Fill your mind with His positive words of health and well-being.*

Be transformed by the renewing of your mind. Then you will be able to test and approve what God's will is—his good, pleasing and perfect will (Rom. 12:2).

30

KNOW WHO YOU ARE

Your thinking needs to be centered not on yourself but on God and who He is and on what He has done for you in Jesus. God calls you not to live in the past but to live in the power of the new life He has given you.

Through what Jesus has done for you on the cross, you are

set free and enabled to live in the glorious liberty of the children of God. You are a new creation, a child of God through faith in Him. God has blessed you in Christ with every spiritual blessing in heaven. He leads you in His triumphal procession. He will meet every need of yours according to His riches in glory in Christ. He has given you everything you need for life and godliness.

YOU ARE IN CHRIST

When you put your faith in Him, God rescued you from the dominion of darkness and brought you into the kingdom of the Son He loves; you are in Christ Jesus, not because you deserve that, but because of God's gracious act, through His love and grace. *You live in Christ, and in Him there is no condemnation, sickness, pain, or disease.*

We all experience such things because we do not live our lives fully in Christ in the way God intends. Because Jesus did His Father's will perfectly, He never succumbed to sin or sickness. To resist sin and sickness, to be more open to the healing power and grace of God, we need to live in the revelation of who we are in Christ. It is not enough just to receive a touch of God's healing in our lives; *He wants to teach us how to live in health and to resist sickness.*

Paul says; "It is because of him [God] that you are in Christ Jesus" (1 Cor. 1:30). You live in Christ; God the Father has placed you in Him because you have put your faith in Him: "And you also were included in Christ when you heard the word of truth, the gospel of your salvation. Having believed, you were marked in him with a seal, the promised Holy Spirit" (Eph. 1:13).

Jesus says, "Remain in me, and I will remain in you" (John 15:4). You live in Jesus and He lives in you. He promises, "If you remain in me and my words remain in you, ask whatever you wish, and it will be given you" (v. 7).

What promises! You are not praying to a distant God. You live in Him and He lives in you. He hears the desires of your heart and knows the thoughts of your mind. He has given you His words and the Holy Spirit to bring those words to life in your heart.

He promises that if His words live in you, you can ask for whatever you want, and it will be given you. He is prepared not only to meet your needs but also to grant the desires of your heart.

It will be given you. Let the promise sink deeply into your heart. *It will be given you.*

How can you be sure you live in Him? John supplies the answer: "We know that we live in him and he in us, because he has given us of his Spirit" (1 John 4:13). You have received the Holy Spirit if you are a born-again believer. This is the very evidence that you live in God and He in you.

God wants you to think of yourself as living in Jesus, not separated from Him, even if at times you do not *feel* very close to Him. He wants you to pray as one confident of your relationship with your heavenly Father.

WALK AS JESUS DID

John writes, "If anyone acknowledges that Jesus is the Son of God, God lives in him and he in God" (1 John 4:15). As a Christian, you believe that Jesus is the Son of God. So you live in Him and He in you.

The Lord wants you to live in a way that reflects these great truths. John declares, "This is how we know we are in him: Whoever claims to live in him must walk as Jesus did" (1 John 2:5–6). You cannot expect to think, pray, believe, and act with the faith of Jesus when needing something from God if, at the same time, you are content to live in a way that is dishonoring to Him. He does not promise to answer your prayers apart from His purpose; He promises to answer them as part of His total purpose in your life.

You have the same power and resources as Jesus had in His humanity. He was able to use those resources fully because He lived in perfect obedience to His Father. That power is diminished in our experience because of our sin and unbelief. If we recognize these things and repent of them, God forgives us, and we find that He is ready to hear our prayers and to answer us because we pray in Jesus' name. We can pray effectively in His name when we are seeking to live in Him, to live as children of His kingdom: "But seek first his kingdom and his righteousness, and all these things will be given to you as well" (Matt. 6:33).

The possibilities are both exciting and limitless. You are not far from Jesus. *You live in Him and He in you.* He has given you the Holy Spirit to enable you to live and to pray in ways that please Him.

He calls you to think and speak about yourself and your circumstances as someone who lives in Him.

IN CHRIST JESUS

It is common for people to be healed of a sense of rejection and personal inadequacy. I wrote *In Christ Jesus* because I was so aware of the need for Christians to see themselves as the new creatures God has made them, set free from their past. There had to be a way of seeing people not only healed of depression but also able to walk in victory. I received this letter concerning that book:

I felt that I must just write to you and encourage you and thank you so much for writing the book *In Christ Jesus*. It has been such a blessing to me, and has transformed my whole outlook on life.

I was a Christian before I read it, and I knew the Word pretty well, but since meditating on the passages and chapters in your book, the effect has been that the Word has begun to be translated from my head to my heart and I am now beginning, at long last, to realize my position *In Christ Jesus*. I have recommended quite a few other Christian friends of mine to read your book and in many cases the effect has been similar. Praise the Lord!

Your book has been the means of giving life to someone who all but died through depression just over a year ago, and who also tried to commit suicide by taking an overdose.

The writer describes three periods of time in a mental hospital:

But praise God, He has graciously reached down and lifted me out of the most terrible darkness I can describe. He has placed my feet on firm ground, and a strong foundation. And now I feel I am beginning to know how to appropriate His Word against the accuser of the brethren; a transformation is gradually taking place in my life, and instead of despair and negative attitudes of hopelessness, which I used to have, these have been replaced by positive assertions of who I am *In Christ Jesus*—and gradually my mind is being renewed and transformed.

I am not completely out of the woods yet, but I know for sure that the Lord has delivered me, and I am learning to stand in my deliverance, and walk in righteousness.

> *God has put you in Christ.*
> *You live in Him.*
> *His words and the Holy Spirit live in you.*
> *You have His promise.*

If you remain in me and my words remain in you, ask whatever you wish, and it will be given you" (John 15:7).

31

RENEW YOUR SPEAKING

The way you speak is an indication of the way you think. Jesus spoke these awesome words: "For by your words you will be acquitted, and by your words you will be condemned" (Matt. 12:37). You can speak negatively or positively. Many people speak themselves into failure, defeat, and even sickness. They concentrate on their symptoms and speak readily about their problems.

This tendency can be seen in an acute form in a person with hypochondria. The person has a constant expectation of sickness because of wrong mental attitudes. God wants you to have the right mental attitudes. He wants you to speak in positive ways that reflect right thinking about yourself in relation to God, in relation to others, and in relation to the whole business of health and wholeness. *Your thinking needs to be in line with God's thinking.* That is another way of saying that your mind needs to be filled with the positive truths of God's Word.

THE HEART SPEAKS

Jesus said, "For out of the overflow of the heart the mouth speaks" (Matt. 12:34). What you believe in your heart affects the way you think and therefore what you say.

When you believe the truth of what God says, your mouth can declare that truth with confidence. Then you will speak faith and act in faith.

It is not what you say in prayer alone that expresses faith or unbelief but what you say in ordinary conversation.

CONFESS THE WORD

To confess the Word is to agree with God and to speak of your circumstances as He would. David learned the importance of speaking the truth to himself:

> Praise the LORD, O my soul,
>   all my inmost being, praise his holy name.
> Praise the LORD, O my soul,
>   and forget not all his benefits (Ps. 103:1–2).

He is speaking to himself, to his own soul. And he continues (vv. 3–5) by giving five good reasons why his confidence should be in God and not his circumstances:

1. *He forgives all my sins.*
2. *He heals all my diseases.*
3. *He redeems my life from the pit.*
4. *He crowns me with love and compassion.*
5. *He satisfies my desires with good things so that my youth is renewed like the eagle's.*

So successful and powerful is confessing the Word in the face of adverse circumstances that David ends the psalm by telling the angels and all the heavenly hosts to join him in praising God!

Declaring the positive truth of His Word and praising Him for who He is direct our attention away from the problem and on to the answer. We are speaking the answer, not the problem.

DON'T UNDERMINE YOUR PRAYERS

Many speak the right faith-sounding words when praying, only to spoil what they have said in ordinary conversation. Whether you are in a position of genuine faith, trusting God for the answer, is determined not so much by the words of your prayers but by what you say about the situation at other times.

At a prayer meeting those who say "Amen" at the end of a prayer do not necessarily believe they have received the answer. If they are in faith, they will speak naturally of that need as if it is already met. They will not continue to speak of the problem; they will rejoice in the answer.

Before praying with someone for healing, I usually ask, "If I pray for you now, what will God do?" It is important to use the method Jesus employed of drawing out a faith response from the person. The answer will indicate the faith expectations.

Saying, "I hope He will heal me," is hope, not faith.

"I really believe; oh, I do believe; I believe He is going to do it. I have such faith and assurance that He is going to heal me" are almost certainly the words of someone trying to convince himself he is in a faith position when he lacks the true revelation of faith in his heart.

"He is going to heal me" is a simple faith statement, and I am happy to proceed with the prayer when I hear such a response.

After praying, I ask, "What has God done for you?" True faith is expressed in the reply, "He has healed me." A person may say this because he knows that all the symptoms have immediately disappeared. It may be he is still conscious of symptoms, but he is appropriating by faith the full measure of healing he needs. But it is important to speak out what he believes.

Notice that I do not tell the person she is healed. She needs to speak out in faith—and to continue to do so until the full healing is manifested.

We are talking not about formulas but about expressing what we believe in our hearts. *Faith will be expressed not only in the prayer meeting but in ordinary conversation.*

CONFLICT AND VICTORY

You can have the early symptoms of a cold or flu. Your nose is blocked, you begin to feel feverish, and perhaps your glands or throat starts to hurt. You can say to yourself, "I am going to get the flu," and the next day you are in bed; your faith has been rewarded. That is what you said to yourself because that is what you believed, so that is what happened. *Negative faith produces negative results.* We are to resist and fight sickness in the name of Jesus: "I reject these symptoms. I'm not going to give in to this in the name of Jesus." You might experience some conflict in your body before experiencing the Lord's victory.

In resisting the enemy's attempts to influence your mind or body, it is important to use the name of Jesus. It is good to speak aloud your rejection of the negative and to use your mouth to praise God for His love, care, and protection. If the battle is His, the victory is His. We are talking not about mind over matter but about the Spirit over mind and matter.

Don't feel condemned if you are not victorious on some occasions. We are all engaged in a faith battle, learning to fight the good fight of faith, learning to proclaim the Lord's victory in the middle of the conflict. Sometimes we receive healing immediately from the Lord; at other times we have to battle through the conflict for hours or even longer.

> *Speak positively about yourself as one who lives in Christ.*
> *The tongue sets the whole course of your life (James 3:6).*
> *Speak positively, not negatively.*
> *Speak health, not sickness.*

The tongue that brings healing is a tree of life (Prov. 15:4).

32

HEALING OF EMOTIONS

Often behind the physical sickness there is emotional need. For example, some people are overweight because they overeat to try to compensate for emotional difficulties or tensions. Others are seriously underweight for similar reasons.

We must take into account the emotional and spiritual factors that often cause physical sickness and stress. God is able to heal people's emotions and free them from everything that binds and restricts them.

THE WAY OF FREEDOM

Having faith in God's Word in your spirit and making the right confession of truth on your lips will bring healing to the emotions as well as to the body. This is not mind over matter but the spirit over mind and matter: "If you hold to my teaching, you are really my disciples. Then you will know the truth, and the truth will set you free" (John 8:31–32). Then Jesus adds, "So if the Son sets you free, you will be free indeed" (v. 36).

You want to be free of physical sickness and emotional need; free of resentment, of fear, of rejection; free to serve the Lord for His praise and honor. *You are set free by discovering not the truth about yourself but the truth about what God has done for you in Jesus.* The work of the Cross meets every spiritual, emotional, and physical need: "Therefore, if anyone is in Christ, he is a new creation; the old has gone, the new has come" (2 Cor. 5:17).

You are not the person you were before you were born again. You have a new nature. Christ lives in you by the presence of the Holy Spirit, and you are being changed from one degree of glory to another—into His likeness. When you see Him face-to-face, you will be like Him. God's purpose of wholeness for you will then be complete.

You are being healed and changed through the truth of what Jesus has done for you. If there is anything from your past that has caused emotional or physical sickness, the Spirit is willing to reveal that the Cross of Jesus has covered that need. Scripture warns us against digging and delving into the past. *You do not need to keep going over the details of the old life in order to be able to live the new.*

If you have a need that is the result of something in your past, this is a present problem. It may be an unresolved conflict or resentment that has been bottled up for years. But the problem is a present one, and forgiveness will be the gateway to the healing, whether emotional, physical, or both.

The basis of *all* divine healing is what God has done for us. Faith enables you to know that you do not have to be a victim of your past. *Christ has set you free to live His new life.*

Often people receive ministry that takes them back farther and farther, reliving the details of their past, because of the lack of faith to believe that Jesus has dealt with these things.

You do not have to relive your past sins before they can be forgiven. You believe that to confess the fact of them is enough to secure God's forgiveness. So why treat sickness any differently when both sin and sickness have been dealt with at the same time—on the cross? *God is equally able to free you from the fact of your emotional need without your having to relive those past experiences. It is His truth that sets you free.*

LISTEN TO THE SPIRIT

The Holy Spirit pinpoints causes of distress and sickness so that you can come to Jesus with repentance and faith. Beware of long prayer sessions, often lasting many hours, in which the details of past events are relived.

Even though I am a new creation now, there may be things from my past that hinder me from living in the victory and power of Jesus in the way He desires. This does not mean God wants me to look back constantly or be turned in upon myself, feeling that I am a victim of my past and unable to live in victory and freedom now. If I have a problem now because of what happened to me in the past, God is able to free me from my problem *now;* all I have to do is identify the problem *now* and allow Him to deal with it.

You do not have to go hunting for the problem; God has given you the Holy Spirit, and He can speak to you about the need in your life or, if you are ministering to others, about the needs in their lives.

Often when I'm praying with someone, God will show me something specific about the person that needs to be dealt with. Such words of knowledge are to be used sensitively. God has provided a key, which can bring His healing into the person's life.

FORGIVE AND BE HEALED

Most emotional need is caused by hurt. Life can be tough; all of us suffer numerous hurts during formative years, and we know how easily we can be hurt still. Some know how to deal with hurt, even of a very traumatic kind; others do not.

The key to the healing of emotional hurt is forgiveness of those who caused the hurt. You will carry the hurt with you until you are prepared to forgive. There is little point in receiving ministry for the healing of an emotional need unless you are willing to forgive.

Once you have forgiven, the way is clear for your healing. You can then invite the Holy Spirit into the wounded areas to bring love, peace, and joy where before there was only pain. Pray for those who hurt you that they may know the Lord's forgiveness, and ask Him to forgive you for the bitterness and resentment that have been stored in your heart toward them, possibly for years.

You will only continue to hurt yourself if you refuse to forgive. That refusal shuts God out of the part of you where you need to receive Him.

We tend to shut off the wounded areas of our lives, enclosing ourselves in emotional shells. Nobody else must touch that raw part because of the pain it will cause. The trouble is that when we build these shells, we shut Jesus out as well as other people.

Forgiveness of those who caused the hurt has the effect of cracking the shell. Then we can allow Jesus to come with the healing touch of the Spirit where before we felt isolated and alone.

Again, you will need to give yourself time to receive healing from Jesus, either alone or with others. So do not be distressed if there are many tears; it is such a relief to allow the Lord to come where previously He was barred. Allow the Holy Spirit to come with the gentleness of His love and peace; He will make you whole! Do not resist Him.

Many people experience resting in the Spirit, especially when they are being healed of emotional need. Jesus promised to give rest to those who came to Him feeling weary and burdened, so we should not be surprised by this phenomenon. The person may be aware of healing and feel completely at peace, knowing Jesus has taken the burdens from him. He may be unaware of healing for some time while he encounters the Lord personally freeing him from deep hurt and bondage.

One thing is certain, if you open the wounded areas of your life to the Lord, having forgiven those who caused the hurt, He will come and heal you, showing you the deep love He has for you.

NO MANIPULATION

Sometimes people have held on to resentment for years; their emotional problems and difficulties have become part of their identity, and they are afraid to release them, even to God. They are afraid they will lose their identity if they do.

Because of their insecurity, they have manipulated others to get attention and affection. What happens if God deals with the need? Does this mean they will no longer receive the same attention? Emotionally immature people are very good at manipulation; they have had a lifetime to practice. Since early childhood, they have become adept at making others do what they ask. Can their manipulative processes be given to God? It is difficult for them to imagine it would be possible to give and receive from others, and from God, without having to manipulate.

Manipulation is not only an indication of emotional inadequacy; it is also the evidence of spiritual insecurity. This insecurity is sickness that God needs to heal. It is impossible to manipulate God; you can never manipulate His love or His healing grace and power.

But Christians are usually easy to manipulate. If someone suggests they are unloving, do not care enough, or have not done enough to help, they are prone to agree and feel guilty. They will then agree to the demands of the manipulator to try to alleviate the sense of failure.

Those who accuse Christians speak in the name of the accuser, Satan, not of God. *Firmly resist such accusations.* It only compounds the problem if you allow insecure people to manipulate you. The loving way is to deal firmly with them. They may threaten reprisals, but most will recognize in you the strength they need, someone who is not so weak as to be easily manipulated.

It is difficult to love manipulators. Yet they may think that the only way they are going to receive love is by continuing to manipulate. If you are prone to manipulating others, realize this: your manipulative processes are preventing you from receiving the real love you want. Bring all your manipulation of others to the Cross, and let God set you free. This freedom will be a most significant healing in your life.

People who manipulate feel sorry for themselves, and *self-pity is one of the most destructive emotions.* It is like a spiritual cancer that destroys faith. Instead of feeling sorry for yourself and thinking that you are the great unloved one who needs to be loved and accepted, you need to believe the truth. God has accepted you in Jesus. You are not rejected. You are able to give to others. When you do, they will start to give to you and love you, not because you manipulate them or make them feel guilty but because they want to.

You are a new creation.
The old has gone; the new has come.
The truth of what Jesus has done for you will bring you
emotional healing.
You do not need to manipulate; Jesus loves you and has
accepted you.

If you hold to my teaching, you are really my disciples. Then you will know the truth, and the truth will set you free (John 8:31–32).

33

COMPASSION, NOT SYMPATHY

Sympathy can be destructive. When people are sick, they are prone to enjoy sympathy. When someone puts an arm around you and says, "Oh, you poor dear," it is tempting to agree and to think, *Here at last is someone who understands how I feel.*

NO SELF-PITY

You never see Jesus sympathizing with people, for sympathy merely compounds their problems. Self-pity is a thing of the flesh, not of the Spirit. Jesus had compassion on people who were sick and healed them. He knew how to take pity on people and show His mercy toward them—not through sympathy (suffering *with* them) but through suffering *for* them on the cross.

We are to weep with those who weep and rejoice with those who rejoice, but that does not mean to compound their problem by saying, "Oh, you poor dear." Rather, we are to point them to the One who carried their burdens for them: "Cast all your anxiety on him because he cares for you" (1 Pet. 5:7).

When David felt sorry for himself, he knew he needed to look away from himself and begin to bless the Lord:

Praise the LORD, O my soul;
　　all my inmost being, praise his holy name.
Praise the LORD, O my soul,
　　and forget not all his benefits—
who forgives all your sins
　　and heals all your diseases (Ps. 103:1–3).

He is speaking to his own soul. He is saying, "David, take your eyes off yourself, off your situation and need. Fix your attention on God. Praise Him for all He has done for you. Let everything in you bless Him. Don't sit around in a cloak of self-pity feeling sorry for yourself. Give to God. Give Him praise, honor, and worship. He is the God who forgives you all your sins, including your self-pity, and who heals all your diseases. You don't have to sit around feeling sorry for yourself because you are sick or have some need. You have the Lord who is the answer to that need. Hallelujah!"

The soul consists of the mind or intellect, the emotions or feelings, and the will. When David says you are to praise the Lord with everything in your soul, with all your inmost being, he includes the emotional part of your life. *Your feelings are not to rule you; they are to be brought under the influence of the Holy Spirit.* The negative feelings will be turned positive only when you look away from yourself to God and praise Him. *Self-pity is destructive of faith because it causes you to concentrate on yourself and the problem instead of on the answer, Jesus.*

Some people imagine their worship to be false if they do not feel like praising God. This is a deception of the enemy to keep them from the very thing they need to do to be liberated from their need. Praise centers on the Lord and the victory He has already won.

BE STRONG

If you are ministering God's grace and love to others, you can point them to the answer, not simply sympathize with them in their need. You are being not harsh but strong! If you are going to help others and minister God's healing to them, you will need to be strong in the way you deal with them. You must be prepared to speak the word from God that they need to hear, even if that is a word of correction or rebuke, or a call to repentance. You are not helping people by avoiding the issue or by being afraid to upset them; you are there to speak the word from God to them. You are called not to take the easy option but to be faithful and true to what God wants you to do by the power of the Spirit.

That does not give you the license to speak to people in judgment and criticism. Speak only in graciousness and love. But do not compromise what needs to be said. If you are not prepared to be faithful, you are likely to hinder the healing process rather than help it.

RECEIVING WHAT GOD SAYS

Always be open to receive and to test what is said when others are ministering to you in the power of the Holy Spirit. Understand that the natural reaction for most people is to reject something about themselves that they do not want to be true. Pray for the Holy Spirit to witness His truth to your heart. Sometimes you need time to absorb what the Lord is saying and to realize its implications. God knows you better than you know yourself.

On one occasion when preaching at an international conference, I needed physical healing. After Communion, opportunity was given for the laying on of hands with prayer. There was no time to make one's personal need known, only to receive prayer briefly. I asked the Lord to make the one praying conscious of my specific need.

When it came to my turn, all he said was, "Father, I ask You to fill Colin with Your peace." I went back to my place disappointed because he had failed to discern my need. But the Lord dealt quickly with me: "He prayed for precisely what you need." I was not conscious of needing peace, but God began to show me that there were areas of tension that lay behind the physical stress in my body. The Lord, through that dear brother, had ministered to me exactly the word I needed to hear, even though it wasn't a word I wanted to hear. I had wanted God to deal only with the physical thing. But God loves us so much He is concerned about our wholeness of mind, body, and spirit.

---

*Jesus loves you and is concerned about your total
   well-being.*
Don't allow emotions and feelings to rule you.
Ask Jesus to forgive any self-pity you may have.
Test what others say to you and respond to what is of God.

It is for freedom that Christ has set us free (Gal. 5:1).

||||||||||||||||||||||||||||||||||||||||||||||||||||||||

Part Six

METHODS OF HEALING

||||||||||||||||||||||||||||||||||||||||||||||||||||||||

34

REPENT AND BELIEVE

There are several different methods of healing demonstrated in the New Testament, all of which need to be used with faith. *A healing method is never a substitute for faith but a means of expressing it.* We shall talk briefly of different ways in which we see the Spirit's healing in the life of the church, in fulfillment of God's Word. These are not the only ways in which God heals, but they are the principal ways in which healing is received by people and through which we can learn to minister healing to one another. You can determine which is the most appropriate means to employ in each situation.

REPENTANCE AND FORGIVENESS

When we come to the Lord to be healed, we come humbly, acknowledging our need and recognizing that we don't deserve anything. We first need to receive forgiveness of our sins because even if the sickness isn't directly caused by sin, unforgiven sin can prevent us from receiving the healing God wants to give. *Receiving God's forgiveness produces immense healing in itself.* Forgiving others has a similar effect, opening the way to receive God's forgiveness and healing.

Somebody with a terminal illness, medically incurable, visited our fellowship in a wheelchair. During the meeting, God convicted the woman of her unwillingness to forgive someone. She repented, asked Him to forgive her, and her healing began from that moment. No one ministered personally to her except the Lord, and within a few weeks she was out of her wheelchair and healed. Such can be the result of giving and receiving forgiveness.

Repentance is not only being forgiven; it also involves the yielding of ourselves to God, particularly if there has been stubborn independence in some area. It involves presenting our bodies to be healed and submitting our lives to the Lord that, as healed people, He may do with us as He pleases.

No matter what other method of healing is employed, it is wise to ensure that first *there are proper repentance and forgiveness from God and toward others.*

Jesus said, "The kingdom of God is near. Repent and believe the good news!" (Mark 1:15).

THE PRAYER OF FAITH

We have already discussed the prayer of faith at length. Whenever Christians have need, they should pray the prayer of faith, putting faith in God, speaking to the mountain, believing they have received what they ask the heavenly Father to do in the name of Jesus. On numerous occasions, especially concerning minor matters, this prayer is all that will be necessary to enable healing.

However, believers are not expected to fight a lonely faith battle; they are members of the household of faith.

It is right to seek help from the body of Christ, employing one or more of the following methods of healing.

Faith does not need others to act as intermediaries, but faith comes often by the fellowship of other believers: "Again, I tell you that if two of you on earth agree about anything you ask for, it will be done for you by my Father in heaven. For where two or three come together in my name, there am I with them" (Matt. 18:19–20).

Even if other methods of healing are used, repentance and faith are always integral to receiving what God wants to give you.

Whenever you turn to the Lord asking Him to meet a need in your life, prepare your heart. Ensure that you know His forgiveness of all your sins and that you have forgiven any who have wronged you.

> *The sacramental acts of healing need to be accompanied by faith.*
> *The spoken words of God that bring healing need to be received with faith.*
> *And the body of Christ, the church, is the household of faith.*

The kingdom of God is near. Repent and believe the good news! (Mark 1:15).

35

THE LAYING ON OF HANDS

The laying on of hands for healing is widely used today, and the method was employed by Jesus and His disciples.

There is nothing magical about hands. Some people claim to have healing properties in their hands; but this is the same kind of claim made by psychic healers, spiritualists, and those involved with the occult. The Christian knows that the healing power is with God. The laying on of hands is an act to be accompanied by faith. It encourages sick persons and those praying with them to believe that at that moment the power of God is being released and liberated into their lives and bodies through the Holy Spirit. This needs to be the expectation of all involved; something definite from God is taking place.

At that moment of contact the power of God has touched their lives; something supernatural has happened to those receiving ministry. They may feel some physical sensation as God's power passes through their bodies, or they may feel nothing. It is not the feelings that matter, but what actually happens as a result of the prayer. If persons believe they have received the healing, whether they feel anything or not, God will honor that faith.

Some may feel heat in their hands as they pray, or they may feel nothing. Such feelings are a poor indication of what is happening. Judge not by physical sensations but by faith in God and His Word. If faith is truly operating, everybody concerned *knows* that the person receiving the laying on of hands is receiving healing from the Lord.

If you receive the laying on of hands, believe that at that moment you are receiving the answer to your need. Believe that the Holy Spirit is coming upon you and is reaching the area of your life where the healing is needed. Believe that you have received it, and it will be yours. This is the promise of Jesus. *When believers believe, believers receive.*

When you lay hands on someone else, believe that Jesus is pouring His healing life into that person at that moment because you are praying in His name, with His authority, and in obedience to His Word. Do not hesitate to believe that God can use you. At first you may feel very tentative in your faith; but if you are prepared to take God at His Word, you will discover that when believers lay hands on people who are sick, "they will get well" (Mark 16:18).

EXPECT RESULTS

Although some people are healed through instantaneous miracles, this is not always the case. In others, the healing may begin to manifest itself after some hours, or even days, if there is faith that the people have received healing from the Lord.

You can lay hands on other members of your family. It is good to ask them to lay hands on you when you have need, parents praying for one another and their children and teaching the children to lay hands on one another and their parents.

But don't allow this to become a matter of routine, an action without faith. Do the work of preparation. Come to God and ask for His forgiveness first. Receive the Word with faith, speak to the mountain, and as you pray, believe that the healing activity and power of God are released at that moment. Do the same in your prayer groups, Bible study groups, or fellowship groups. Do it in your congregation, in every place where God's people meet together in the name of Jesus. This is an opportunity to minister God's love and grace to one another by the power of the Holy Spirit.

Once again, avoid allowing the laying on of hands to become a mechanical action. Little will happen if you do. It is not glorifying to the Lord or helpful to the people concerned if nothing happens because there is no genuine faith that expects God's power to be at work supernaturally.

> *As a believer, you can lay hands on sick people.*
> *When believers believe, believers receive.*

They will place their hands on sick people, and they will get well (Mark 16:18).

36

ANOINTING WITH OIL

The command in James 5 is for "any one of you" (v. 14) who is sick to call for the elders of the church. Any means *any*. God's expectation is that there will be such faith in the local congregation that if *any* Christian is sick, he will call the elders or leaders of his fellowship to pray and anoint him in the name of Jesus.

There is nothing to indicate that it was a temporary command for apostolic times. It is the word of the Lord for today, as for every other day.

The healing is not in the oil, just as the healing is not in the hands laid on a person's head. The healing is in God and is released through faith. The anointing with oil is a way of stimulating faith. The disciples "anointed many sick people with oil and healed them" (Mark 6:13).

We cannot escape the fact that this practice has fallen into disuse in many churches because of unbelief. There is an absence of obedience to the Word because there is an absence of faith that if the Word is obeyed, healing will occur.

JAMES 5

The sequence of events in James, chapter 5, is significant:

- James addresses any who are sick.
- The sick Christian has the responsibility to call for the

elders of the church. It is not the duty of the elders to call on the Christian and suggest that he be anointed. *The sick person needs to express faith and obedience by calling for the elders.*

- He is asking not for a social visit but for prayer and anointing, "to pray over him and anoint him with oil in the name of the Lord" (v. 14). *He is expecting to be healed as a result.*

- The anointing is not a mechanical act, for "the prayer offered in faith will make the sick person well" (v. 15). James thereby puts the emphasis on the faith of those present. The anointing with oil (a biblical symbol of God's Spirit) stimulates that faith and enables them to believe that the healing power of God's Spirit is pouring into the sick person at that moment. Oil is also the symbol of consecration to the Lord's purposes. The sick one desires healing that his life be used fruitfully as one consecrated to the Lord.

- The promise of God is that "the Lord will raise him up" (v. 15).

- Confession of sin and forgiveness for the sick person accompany the anointing. We have discussed these important parts of the process of healing.

- James urges open confession of sins. It is often helpful (sometimes essential) for the sick person to bring into the light what has been hidden in the dark.

- The expectation of God's Word is clear: "Therefore confess your sins to each other and pray for each other so that you may be healed" (v. 16). Healing is expected.

- It is appropriate for those praying to prepare through confession of sins and forgiveness, for then they are cleansed of all unrighteousness. James emphasizes that "the prayer of a righteous man is powerful and effective" (v. 16). There is little point in trying to pray with faith if you know there is any deliberate unrighteousness in your life.

- All involved are to pray earnestly, like Elijah. Anointing is not to be administered with a doubting attitude: "Let's try this and hope that it works." *If there is faith, the elders will pray earnestly, confident of God's faith fulness.*

We need to remember that the Lord regards healing as part of the responsibility of those exercising pastoral leadership over His children. According to God's Word, every pastor and elder is to have a healing ministry.

Obey God's Word.
Call for the elders when necessary.
Expect to receive your healing.

And the prayer offered in faith will make the sick person well (James 5:15).

37

HOLY COMMUNION

Paul says, "For whenever you eat this bread and drink this cup, you proclaim the Lord's death until he comes" (1 Cor. 11:26). Holy Communion is a proclamation of all Jesus has done for us on the cross, giving His body and pouring out His blood that we might be saved from sin, sickness, and eternal death.

Every time we share in these gifts, we recall and are able to receive afresh the full significance of Jesus' sacrifice made for us on the cross. It is common to hear preaching about the virtue of the Lord's blood: "This is my blood of the covenant, which is poured out for many for the forgiveness of sins" (Matt. 26:28). But very little is said about the gift of His body.

Jesus gave His body to the smiters so that by His wounds we may be healed. There has been much faith in the church for the forgiveness of sins but little for the healing that comes through the stripes Jesus bore on His body.

The seeds of this unbelief existed among the Corinthian Christians. Paul tells them, "Anyone who eats and drinks without recognizing the body of the Lord eats and drinks judgment on himself. That is why many among you are weak and sick, and a number of you have fallen asleep" (1 Cor. 11:29–30).

RELEVANCE TO TODAY

Are many members of churches today weak and sick? Do we see some dying of disease? The answer to both questions is obviously yes. What Paul is saying to the Corinthians is directly relevant to the church today.

What is the cause of this sickness and death? People are eating and drinking unworthily, without discerning the *body* of the Lord. If there is little faith, people will approach holy Communion carelessly. If they believe that God is offering the full virtue of the Cross, healing and wholeness of body, soul, and spirit, they will come suitably prepared.

I have learned to say something like this when receiving the bread: "Lord, I believe that as I eat this bread, I have received all the virtue of Christ's body. I thank You for the physical strength and healing I receive through His stripes. I thank You for the material and financial provision I have for all my needs through His abundant grace." If there is particular healing I need, I pray the prayer of faith and believe that I receive healing from the Lord.

When receiving the cup, I say, "Thank You, Father, for the blood of Jesus through which I have received forgiveness of all my sins and deliverance from all evil. Thank You that He has made me holy and righteous in Your sight so that I can live the new life You have given me."

BELIEFS

Different people have different beliefs about this sacrament. Those who regard it as a memorial need to have a living faith in what is commemorated, the Cross of Jesus Christ. As they receive the bread and cup, they need to rejoice that they are healed and made whole through His sacrifice at Calvary.

Some people believe that at the moment of receiving the gifts, they are receiving afresh the virtue of the Cross—strength and healing for the body and cleansing of the soul.

Others believe in the real presence of body and blood; they believe that Jesus is really present in the sacrament to give His healing and forgiveness.

It does not matter essentially *how* you believe but *what* you believe and that you come suitably prepared to receive the healing and forgiveness made possible through the Father's gift of His Son on the cross.

Paul says, "But if we judged ourselves, we would not come under judgment" (1 Cor. 11:31). His words seem to indicate that to Paul, much of the sickness and death among the church members could be avoided if only they searched their hearts diligently and came to the Lord with repentance,

knowing His grace, mercy, and love in His willingness to
forgive and make them whole.

If you want to appropriate healing through holy Communion, prepare as thoroughly as you would if asking for the
laying on of hands or anointing.

---

*Every time you participate in holy Communion, you
share a means of God's grace to you.*

*This can be an occasion when your faith is expressed,
believing Him to pour His healing life into you
spiritually, emotionally, and physically.*

*To receive holy Communion in the way Paul indicates is
the best preventive medicine.*

Jesus will keep you in health.

This is my body, which is [broken] for you (1 Cor. 11:24).

38

HEALING THROUGH HEARING

A WORD OF FAITH OR REVELATION

People are often healed while reading the Scriptures or hearing the Word of God preached. A particular Scripture verse is
brought as revelation to the heart by the Holy Spirit. It is as if
there is a sudden leap of faith with the sick person, who

knows that she is healed. The healing is very simple when it happens like that.

Preaching that emphasizes the healing work of the Cross, or demonstrates from God's Word that it is His will to heal, frequently has the same result. No doubt many will be healed while reading this book because it simply opens their hearts to the truth of God's Word.

As part of our ministry, we make available free of charge the Kingdom Faith Teaching Course. It is a series of cassettes on each of which are four twenty-minute talks that can be used in a group or in a private session, one talk per week. One of these cassettes is on healing, and we have received many letters saying that people have been healed as a result of listening to it. The proclamation of God's Word has brought revelation. One letter told of this incident:

> I thank and praise God for the blessings we are continually receiving through them [the tapes]. We experienced yet another miraculous healing. A woman of around sixty was suffering from arthritis and she was having difficulty accepting that the Lord could heal her. We were discussing praying for her when all of a sudden she said, "Yes! I can see it now. He can heal me." She had no sooner said it, than her right leg (which was locked and swollen) started tingling and she was healed. The leg was unlocked and the swelling disappeared.

When people are healed in this way, there is no prayer, no speaking to God. He has spoken to the people who are sick, and their response is a joyful thanksgiving to Him. You can see why there has been so much emphasis in this book on hearing and believing Scripture. The more you read the Bible, the more opportunity you give the Holy Spirit to witness the truth of His Word to you so that you receive the spirit, life, and healing in the Word.

I have lost count of the number of testimonies I have heard from people seriously ill, often near death, who have experienced the Spirit bringing to their hearts the truth: "By his wounds you have been healed" (1 Pet. 2:24). In their weakness they believe and immediately begin to recover.

Usually, no human intermediary is needed in this method of God's healing grace. The sick person hears the Lord as he reads Scripture, prays, or lies in bed ill. Sometimes the words of healing may be spoken by another often without realization of the significance of what has been said. There have been occasions when God has simply laid a verse of Scripture on my heart to speak. Later I have been told that the person was too sick to hear or understand anything else that was said. Those few words from the Lord were enough and brought him through to healing.

A WORD OF KNOWLEDGE OR AUTHORITY

Peter used a word of knowledge or authority when healing the beggar at the temple gate: "In the name of Jesus Christ of Nazareth, walk" (Acts 3:6). This fulfills the Lord's command to His church to heal sick people in His name—not simply pray for them. It is exercising the authority given to believers and fulfilling the commission to the church.

If it was a method of communicating healing used by Jesus and the early disciples, we should expect to see it still in use today because the same Holy Spirit is at work to bring God's power into the lives of His people.

There are three necessary ingredients for this method of healing to be used effectively:

1. *Revelation must be received by the person speaking the word* that this is a particular moment when God's healing power is to be received by someone. Presumably, Peter had passed the beggar many times. It was the moment for his

healing. Jesus did not go to all sick people and speak healing to them, but He healed those who came to Him.

2. *Faith is present* in the one who speaks the word and often, but not always, in the one who hears. There is nothing to indicate that either the beggar at the temple gate or the man at the Pool of Bethesda to whom Jesus spoke was a believer. Even so, both men responded to the words of command spoken to them.

3. *The words are spoken with authority*, and so the power of God accomplishes what is said. The one who speaks can exercise that authority if he has received revelation of what God desires to do and has faith that He will do it.

PUBLIC USE OF THIS GIFT

At large public meetings, I find this to be the most fruitful way of ministering Jesus' healing power. Many hundreds of people can receive healing in a very short space of time. Time would not permit individual laying on of hands for such numbers, and it can be more effective to hear a word from God concerning your personal need.

This is not to say that others are not involved in the ministry. It is good for everybody present to lay hands on one another or to link hands so that the whole body of people present is involved.

Usually, before these words of knowledge for healing, the people have heard the gospel preached; they have quickened their faith, even if there has been no direct mention of healing; and they have been led through a time of repentance. Sins have been forgiven, and they have had the opportunity of making a fresh consecration of their lives to the Lord. During that time, there may be words of knowledge about specific areas of sin in those present. Words of knowledge are not confined to physical healing.

After taking authority over the enemy and binding every spirit of infirmity and sickness, we can speak to the mountains and command them to be moved in the name of Jesus. The Holy Spirit will then make me aware of particular needs that are being met at that moment. The words of knowledge will then be spoken with authority, and the healing will take place. That may seem simple, and it is when God's children are moving in revelation received from the Spirit. Incurable diseases can be instantly healed as people receive personally from the Lord the words spoken to them.

THE RESULTS

When first using this method of healing, I made careful inquiries of many hundreds, even thousands, of people to discover what happened to them.

Some already had faith, confident that it was the moment they would receive healing. The word spoken was confirmation of the belief and released their faith to receive from God.

Some were less confident, but the word spoken created faith, and they reached out to receive from God.

Some did not have faith and may not have been thinking of their own needs because they were busy praying for others. For them, there came the sudden realization that God had spoken to them and met their need.

There were various ways in which the healing took place. Some were instantly healed the moment the words were spoken. Others knew that a healing process had begun, although they had not previously believed it was God's purpose to heal them. For others, the word came as a promise to be appropriated by faith. As they held on to that word in the days ahead, thanking God for His healing, they experienced His power at work within them.

Some words were general and applied to several people at

the same time. Others were very specific and could be meant only for a particular individual.

It is not only at large public gatherings where certain people minister that this gift is used. It is a gift for the whole body. A word of knowledge can be received by one member of a prayer group, and when spoken out, another person present can receive healing.

However, it must be emphasized that this gift begins with revelation from the Spirit. It is not a question of going to every sick person and saying, "Be healed in the name of Jesus," or to every person in a wheelchair and saying, "Get up and walk." People can be confused if they listen to their emotions rather than to the voice of the Spirit.

Let us also understand that a word of knowledge or authority does not indicate that God *wants* to heal. We know it is His will to heal, and we need no special word from God for that. *This is a word of revelation indicating that God's healing purpose is being realized in a particular person or people at that moment.*

I am often staggered at the number of people who receive healing within a few minutes through others speaking out words of knowledge and authority. It may be right to pray further with some, but usually, the healing has already begun as a result of the word being spoken and received.

It is important for people to speak out what they believe has happened to them. I may ask people to testify briefly so that all can hear or come to me to tell me of the healings received or, in the case of large meetings, share with those around them what God has done for them.

Sometimes people are so conscious of symptoms that they doubt their healing at that moment. But within a few days, without being conscious of what happened to them at the meeting, they realize that God has touched them with His healing power.

This is a method of healing being widely restored to the church today, sometimes in conjunction with one of the other methods, such as the laying on of hands. A certain boldness of faith is being restored as the Spirit deals with the unbelief among God's people. God witnessed to my heart, "Colin, if you dare to speak it, I will do it." It is easier to speak some things than others, but I know the truth of what the Lord has said. In this way I have known Him to heal a great variety of diseases from minor complaints to terminal illnesses such as cancer and multiple sclerosis. The power is with God, and all things are equally simple to the one who is the Almighty. John's healing reported in chapter 1 of this book is one example. Here is another, the healing of someone not even present at the meeting itself:

> A few weeks before the mission to Luton a friend of one of our members was told that her daughter, Hazel, aged seven, had an inoperable brain tumor and was given two years to live. . . .
>
> As Colin was telling of healings for people in the crowd, he then said that he saw a brain tumor being healed and that the person concerned may not be present. . . .
>
> We have now heard—Oh praise God—that she has recently had a brain-scan and there is no sign of any tumor—or any trace as to where it was—the surgeon told her that she was making medical history—they say they have no medical explanation—but we have the explanation—we know of the Father's power that works only in love—and of this ministry of healing that is here in our world today.

We have to be sensitive to the Spirit's voice, listening to what He is saying, and ready to speak out what He gives us to speak.

It is always a particular joy when I receive a word that releases others into ministry. For example, there was once a word that someone present should go and pray with a blind person of his acquaintance. A man, who had been a Christian for only a few weeks, knew that direction was for him. His friend had been born blind in one eye and had gone blind in the other. He obediently went and prayed with him. As a result, God restored sight to both eyes.

When you minister personally to others, there will be times when you will not be sure exactly what is being received at that moment. On other occasions you will know even before you pray with a person that he is going to be healed there and then, no matter how serious his condition. Having received that revelation, you can pray and speak with faith and authority.

> *Listen to the Lord in His Word.*
> *Listen to the voice of the Spirit.*
> *Jesus wants to speak His words of healing to you.*

Just say the word, and my servant will be healed (Matt. 8:8).

39

COUNSELING HINTS

When people come to you for counsel, they do not need loads of good advice from you; they need a word from God they have not been able to hear for themselves.

Counseling is much in vogue these days. The Holy Spirit is the Counselor, and any valid counseling ministry will be exercised in the power of the Holy Spirit. We cannot attempt a full discussion of this subject here but will point briefly to a few important factors concerned with counseling people for healing:

- *A good counselor will listen* but will not allow the person to repeat himself continually, going over his problems again and again.
- *Discern where the person is in her faith.* Is there any expectation that God will meet the need? If not, you will need to open up the Scriptures briefly, praying that the Word will be received with revelation.
- The counselor can know the answer to the person's problems; but *that person needs to see the answer for himself or receive it as revelation from God.*
- *One sentence from God can accomplish more than a whole book from a man or a woman.* Pray that God will give you the word that comes from Him and that will be received as revelation by the person you are seeking to help.
- *Move into prayer as soon as possible,* having allowed the person to vocalize the need. More will be accomplished in prayer than in hours of discussion.
- *Do not do the other person's praying for her.* Let her bring herself and her need to the Lord, conscious that she is casting the burden on Him so that she will not have to carry the weight of it any longer.
- *Give assurance of God's acceptance and forgiveness.* In nearly every case in which people ask for counsel, you will find they lack assurance.
- *Pray in the Spirit.* Expect God to speak through you prophetically, and do not hold back from speaking out

what you believe He is saying. His word is "sharper than any double-edged sword, it penetrates even to dividing soul and spirit... judges the thoughts and attitudes of the heart" (Heb. 4:12). Remember it is the one sentence from God that can change a person's life, bringing the revelation and healing needed.

- Whatever the problem exposed, *encourage the person to understand the need has already been met in Christ.*
- *Impress upon the person the need to obey any directive word God has given him by the Spirit.* Failure to obey will result in his remaining in the same place as before, and he is likely to be back for more help before long.
- *Send the person away in faith, thanking God* for the healing received, with the determination to maintain positive confession that her needs are met in Jesus.

These are hints and do not constitute a formula for counseling. Above all, remember that *the answer to the need is not in the person but in Christ.* You will have to counteract the natural tendency for people to look in upon themselves, to analyze themselves and search for reasons why they should not be healed. Faith in what Jesus has done is the object of the exercise. The person before you needs to hear the sentence or few sentences that will build faith and release God's healing power into the situation. It may be a word of revelation that brings conviction of sin and repentance, but response to that word begins the process of healing.

When counseling, expect God to give you words of knowledge and of wisdom as necessary.
You are ministering healing in the name of Jesus and with the power of the Holy Spirit.
Be as direct and positive as possible.

So if the Son sets you free, you will be free indeed (John 8:36).

40

LOVE IN THE BODY OF CHRIST

Any loving congregation is supposed to be a fellowship of believers in whom the Spirit of love dwells, who are committed to loving one another as Christ has loved them, and who are ready to face the cost of reaching out to lost, sick, and seemingly unlovable people with the love of God.

The New Testament knows nothing of churchgoers or attenders; every Christian is a member of the body of Christ and has clear-cut responsibilities, especially in the area of loving others.

ACCEPTED AND LOVED

Many emotional needs, which often underlie physical needs, come from a sense of rejection or unworthiness. People feel they are unloved, inferior, and unwanted. They need to know God's love for them. Simply telling them they are loved is insufficient; that love needs to be demonstrated. They need to be shown that they are accepted and helped to see that they can be fruitful and useful members of the fellowship.

With some needs, it is inadequate to pray with someone

and then send him back into the situation that may have caused, or at least aggravated, his condition. Sometimes Christians need to face the cost of opening their homes and inviting people to live with them. That is a very costly kind of love, but there are certain kinds of emotional need that can be met fully only in this way.

Jesus demonstrated His care for His mother while hanging on the cross: "When Jesus saw his mother there, and the disciple whom he loved standing nearby, he said to his mother, 'Dear woman, here is your son,' and to the disciple, 'Here is your mother.' From that time on, this disciple took her into his home" (John 19:26–27). Jesus counteracted the problem of loneliness even before the need arose.

During a twelve-year-period, my family and I had over sixty different people living with us for prolonged periods of time, many of them emotionally needy people. We know well the demands of such ministry, which draws out from within you the resources of God's love, and we did this within the context of an extremely busy ministry. But it is rewarding to see people grow in freedom, security, and responsibility.

LOVE—THE BASIS OF MINISTRY

Nobody can have a healing ministry unless it has the love of Jesus as its foundation. Those who want power and glory will be sadly deficient without learning to demonstrate God's love by the Holy Spirit.

But love is the responsibility of the whole body of Christ. It is amazing how many excuses Christians can find to help them avoid the more costly responsibilities. It is extremely costly to help people with addictions to drugs or alcohol in the name of Jesus. Many with lesser problems need Christian homes where there is an atmosphere of love and faith in which they can be healed of their insecurities. You do not need to have a healing ministry for that to happen; only be willing to love.

There will be many disappointments when your love is thrown back in your face and people succumb to the great temptation to turn back to the life that has almost destroyed them. It is easy to recognize your own inadequacy in such ministry but at the same time to wonder at how love so often prevails where all else seems to have failed.

It is not a question of love or faith but of realizing that "the only thing that counts is faith expressing itself through love" (Gal. 5:6). Certainly, there is no better way of learning how to minister to people than to live with them! However, it is important to distinguish between those who would like you to support them in their needs and those who are genuinely concerned to see the Lord meet their needs so that they can lead useful, fruitful lives. It is also necessary to understand that wisdom is needed. Some people are so demanding in the early stages of sorting out their lives that they would tear the life of a family apart in no time. Community or healing households with several Christian adults are indicated if such needs are to be ministered to effectively.

This book is not the place for a lengthy discussion of this type of healing ministry. All Christians need to understand that their homes belong to the Lord. If it is not practicable for people to live with them, at least they can have an open house to one or two lonely people or to those weak in faith who need encouragement.

The idea is not to make people dependent on you but to give them a sense of belonging to a Christian family where they know they are loved, accepted, and encouraged to be useful, productive members of the body of Christ.

There is nothing great or wonderful about our home. We

are simply a group of people seeking to live together in the love of Jesus, and we are prepared to open our hearts, our home, and our lives to share them with others. Whatever healing the Lord does in all of us is by His grace alone.

There should not be loneliness or a sense of rejection within any Christian fellowship. Surely, God wants to see the modern equivalent of the New Testament experience: "All the believers were one in heart and mind. No one claimed that any of his possessions was his own, but they shared everything they had . . . much grace was upon them all. There were no needy persons among them" (Acts 4:32–34). It was within the context of such love, faith, and commitment that God moved so powerfully.

METHODS

One of the most perplexing things, some people would say one of the most difficult things, about the healing ministry is that there is no set formula for healing. You cannot produce a pattern and say, "If you do 1, 2, 3, 4, 5, you will automatically receive your healing." You cannot minister to one person as you would to another. Every situation is different, every person unique. You cannot pray with B in the same way as with A, nor with C in the same way as with B. In each situation you have to be guided by the Holy Spirit. It is very important to be a listening person, sensitive to the voice of the Spirit and willing to use whatever method is appropriate, to be open for God to speak to you and to guide you step-by-step in each case. You will learn certain principles of the kingdom that apply universally, but you will need to avoid establishing any system of healing.

> *Jesus is love.*
> *Jesus loves you.*
> *You can bring healing into others' lives through love.*

My command is this: Love each other as I have loved you (John 15:12).

Part Seven

DELIVERANCE

41

GOD OUR DELIVERER

Deliverance is a word used in different ways by different people. In the Old Testament, it is used to show how God delivered His people from their enemies:

> From the LORD comes deliverance (Ps. 3:8).

> You are my hiding place;
>   you will protect me from trouble
>   and surround me with songs of deliverance (Ps. 32:7).

> You will not have to fight this battle. Take up your positions; stand firm and see the deliverance the LORD will give you, O Judah and Jerusalem. Do not be afraid; do not be discouraged. Go out to face them tomorrow, and the LORD will be with you (2 Chron. 20:17).

The Lord was angry when His people "did not believe in God or trust in his deliverance" (Ps. 78:22). Certainly, He gives promises to His people that He will save and deliver them from their enemies. In Scripture, the king of Babylon is seen as a type of the devil himself. "Do not be afraid of the king of Babylon, whom you now fear. Do not be afraid of him, declares the LORD, for I am with you and will save you and deliver you from his hands" (Jer. 42:11).

DELIVERED FROM EVIL

God delivers His people from every form of evil because He is their deliverer. It is His nature to deliver them:

> The LORD is my rock, my fortress and my deliverer (Ps. 18:2).

> O Sovereign LORD, my strong deliverer,
> who shields my head in the day of battle (Ps. 140:7).

So we should expect Jesus to deliver God's people from all the powers of the devil, their spiritual enemy, and from every form of evil. "Deliver us from evil" is a phrase from the prayer Jesus taught His disciples. Paul wrote, "And having disarmed the powers and authorities, he made a public spectacle of them, triumphing over them by the cross" (Col. 2:15).

Paul speaks of the Lord delivering him from the deadly dangers encountered through opposition to his ministry: "He has delivered us from such a deadly peril, and he will deliver us. On him we have set our hope that he will continue to deliver us" (2 Cor. 1:10).

FREED FROM THE ENEMY

Deliverance, therefore, is the activity of God that frees people from the powers of the enemy, from Satan and his demonic forces. The greatest act of deliverance happens at new birth, when God rescues new Christians "from the dominion of darkness" and brings them "into the kingdom of the Son he loves" (Col. 1:13). However, the word *deliverance* is generally used today in two specific instances:

1. The act of setting free someone possessed by a demon.

2. The act of freeing a person from oppression by the powers of darkness.

There is a clear distinction between *possession* and *oppression*.

> *The Lord is your deliverer.*
> *He has rescued you from the dominion of darkness.*
> *He has brought you into His kingdom.*
> *He has freed you from all the powers of the enemy.*

From the LORD comes deliverance (Ps. 3:8).

42

JESUS DELIVERS THE POSSESSED

On several occasions, Jesus sets people free from demonic possession. It is not the devil who possesses people, but his evil spiritual beings called demons. (The King James Version translation *devils* is an incorrect rendering of the Greek. There is only one devil, but there are many demons.) The devil himself entered Judas Iscariot before he betrayed Jesus; it was Satan himself who controlled Judas in that treacherous act. The situation was exceptional because it was the climax of the great conflict between Satan and God's Son, ultimately resulting in Jesus' victory on the cross.

Jesus healed many who were possessed not by the devil but by demons, who are the agents or forces of the devil. They are spiritual personalities or beings who recognize the devil as their master. They want bodies in which to live so that they can manipulate the people and use them to manifest their evil characters.

People can be possessed by several demons. When Jesus cast the demons out of one man, they went into a whole herd of pigs that ran into the water and drowned (Mark 5:1–13). Jesus set Mary Magdalene free from seven demons (Luke 8:2). Some demonic forces created mental disturbance; others caused physical sickness or disabilities, as with the demon-possessed boy without the power of speech and the boy with epilepsy, both of whom were healed by Jesus.

The demon exerts a power over the person who, when possessed, is powerless to resist this evil activity. Consequently, when Jesus ministered to people who were possessed, He did not ask for a response of faith from them as He did from those who came to Him for healing. The demon had control over the person and would not want to cooperate.

DEMONS RECOGNIZE JESUS' AUTHORITY

However, the demons recognized Jesus as God's Son and were frightened of His authority. *They knew that He had power over them, and that if He commanded them to leave a person, they had to obey.*

Sometimes Jesus prevented the demons from saying publicly that He was the Messiah. He did not want such a declaration to come from demonic forces at the wrong time.

When delivering possessed people, Jesus commanded the demons to leave, and immediately, the people were set free. When healing the boy with epilepsy, "Jesus rebuked the demon, and it came out of the boy, and he was healed from that moment" (Matt. 17:18).

A man in the synagogue at Capernaum "cried out at the top of his voice, 'Ha! What do you want with us, Jesus of Nazareth? Have you come to destroy us? I know who you are—the Holy One of God!' 'Be quiet!' Jesus said sternly. 'Come out of him!' Then the demon threw the man down before them all and came out without injuring him" (Luke 4:33–35).

The demons had to obey Jesus when He spoke with authority to them, a fact that impressed the people: "With authority and power he gives orders to evil spirits and they come out!" (Luke 4:36).

The Jewish leaders accused Jesus of being demon-possessed Himself and of casting out demons by Beelzebub, the prince of demons. They could not understand how He could demonstrate such power over evil forces. Jesus replied, "I am not possessed by a demon... but I honor my Father and you dishonor me. I am not seeking glory for myself" (John 8:49–50). Others recognized that no demon-possessed man could do the things Jesus did.

Jesus came to set captives free and demonstrated that it was His Father's will to deliver those who were bound by Satan: "When evening came, many who were demon-possessed were brought to him, and he drove out the spirits with a word and healed all the sick" (Matt. 8:16). This healing, Matthew says, Jesus did to demonstrate that He took our infirmities and carried our diseases.

Mark tells us that Jesus "drove out many demons, but he would not let the demons speak because they knew who he was" (Mark 1:34). At Nazareth during the early days of His ministry, Jesus quoted the opening verses of Isaiah, chapter 61, stating that this Scripture was to be fulfilled in Him: "He has sent me to proclaim freedom for the prisoners and recov-

ery of sight for the blind, to release the oppressed, to proclaim the year of the Lord's favor" (Luke 4:18–19).

AUTHORITY GIVEN TO JESUS' DISCIPLES

*Jesus gave the same authority and power over demons to the
disciples.* He told them to "drive out demons" (Matt. 10:8).
They had freely received the gift of God's kingdom. *They
could bring freedom to others by exercising the authority of
God's reign over the powers of darkness:* "When Jesus had
called the Twelve together, he gave them power and authority
to drive out all demons and to cure diseases, and he sent
them out to preach the kingdom of God and to heal the sick"
(Luke 9:1–2).

That authority was not confined to the Twelve. After the
seventy-two disciples had been sent out, they "returned with
joy and said, 'Lord, even the demons submit to us in your
name'" (Luke 10:17). Of all that they had seen happening,
that authority caught their attention most. But Jesus is quick
to teach them an important truth: "I saw Satan fall like
lightning from heaven. I have given you authority to trample
on snakes and scorpions and to overcome all the power of the
enemy; nothing will harm you. However, do not rejoice that
the spirits submit to you, but rejoice that your names are
written in heaven" (Luke 10:18–20).

It was not the fact of the demons submitting to them that
was to be the cause for joy but the reason that they had to
submit to them. Satan was thrown out of heaven when he
rebelled against God's authority. He and all his demonic
spirits do not belong where the disciples of Jesus belong.
Christians belong to the kingdom of God; their names are
written in heaven. *Because they are part of God's sovereign
rule, they have authority over every power that belongs to the
enemy.*

> *Jesus has power and authority over all demonic powers.*
> *Jesus gives this power and authority to His disciples.*
> *Your name is written in heaven.*
> *He gives you this same power and authority.*

I tell you the truth, whatever you bind on earth will be bound in heaven, and whatever you loose on earth will be loosed in heaven (Matt. 18:18).

43

AUTHORITY GIVEN TO BELIEVERS

Deliverance is part of the ministry of those who belong to God's kingdom and is not confined to those first disciples. Jesus says that anyone with faith will do the same things that He did. When giving His commission to the church, He said, "And these signs will accompany those who believe: In my name they will drive out demons" (Mark 16:17).

MODERN ERROR

Some modern thinkers suggest that demons do not exist. If people do not believe in a real devil, it is only logical that they will not believe in demonic powers, either. They say that Jesus used such language only because belief in demons was popular in His day. He was using the language of the people.

Such suggestions are both heretical and blasphemous. They suggest that Jesus deliberately deceived people. Yet He contested common misunderstandings throughout His teaching. Why should demons be an exception? And why should Jesus address demons if they did not exist?

These ideas say that Jesus was Himself deceived in this matter, which would make Him imperfect and a victim of Satan the deceiver, thus making it impossible for Him to be the Lamb without blemish, who offered His perfect life on the cross for the sin of the whole world.

Or these thinkers say that Jesus knew the truth but deliberately deceived the people by going along with their ideas. Deception is the work of the devil, and to accuse Jesus of deliberate deception is blasphemous.

Anyone who has a personal relationship with Jesus Christ knows the reality of the devil's existence. And anyone who has been involved in the healing ministry knows that demons are real enough.

DISCERNMENT NEEDED

Failure to recognize the presence of demonic possession has left many people bound mentally and physically. This is not to say that all mental disease is the result of possession or that all physical disease is the direct work of demons. But some mental and physical sickness is certainly the result of demonic possession, as Jesus clearly shows.

He did not always address demons when healing people who were sick. But when they were the source of the problem, He commanded them to leave with authority, and people were immediately delivered both spiritually and physically. He knew that to pray for healing would not have been effective in such circumstances. *Demons are to be commanded, not prayed for.*

Discernment is needed to determine whether the nature of a person's sickness is demonic and whether deliverance needs to be exercised. This is not to say that people are to go to extremes and imagine that demons are lurking behind every tree. There is no deliverance ministry separate from the ministry of healing; the one is part of the other. Jesus holds both in the correct balance.

When a person is possessed, a demon lives within and can control that person, at least in part. The demon may cause the inability to speak, epilepsy, or some other physical disease; or it may take over the person's personality in some way, forcing him to do things he does not want to do. Certain types of mental sickness are caused by possession by demonic forces, and the reason why some mental problems do not respond to medical treatment is therefore obvious. There is no medical cure for demon-possession. Many psychiatrists do not even believe in the existence of demons.

In the healing ministry, you will inevitably have to exercise authority over demons on occasion. A failure to do so will leave the person in bondage. One of the gifts of the Holy Spirit is the ability to distinguish between spirits. God wants us to listen very carefully to Him and to perceive whether something is the result of physical or emotional stress or whether there is demonic activity that needs to be dealt with. *As believers, we do not need to fear demons; we are given power and authority over them by the Lord.*

A possessed person is incapable of breaking free from what possesses her. She needs somebody else to deliver her by exercising authority in the name of Jesus. Jesus told the disciples that whatever they bound on earth was bound in heaven and that whatever they loosed on earth was loosed in heaven. When so bound, Satan is unable to hinder the deliverance and subsequent healing.

When I pray for people with illnesses, I habitually bind

the enemy whether there is any demonic possession involved or not. Then the devil is rendered powerless to resist the healing work of God in the people's lives. *The idea of being able to plunder Satan's goods puts us in the right faith position, knowing we have power and authority over all his works.*

There are times when we have to be defensive against the enemy's attack on us; but there are other occasions when we need to be on the offensive, boldly proclaiming the victory of Jesus over all the powers of Satan. We can say, "Satan, you are bound in the name of Jesus, and we are going to plunder your goods." Before speaking at a public meeting, I bind the enemy like this because during that meeting, people will come to know the Lord, they will be baptized in the Holy Spirit, and many will be healed. Some will need to be set free and delivered, and Satan is not allowed to intervene.

NO NEED TO FEAR

Christians should not be afraid of the enemy. *Satan is afraid of believers who know their kingdom rights and who exercise the power and authority given them in the name of Jesus.* Before your new birth, you were in Satan's kingdom, and he was able to kick you about and use you to oppose God's purposes. Now that you belong to God's kingdom, you have power and authority over Satan.

This does not mean you are called to a particular ministry of delivering possessed people. It is better to leave that to individuals with experience in such matters. But if you find yourself in a position where somebody is manifesting obvious signs of demon-possession and there is no one else readily available, you may need to exercise the power and authority given you as a child of God.

We need to respect that these forces can be extremely powerful and sometimes violent, but we still do not need to be afraid "because the one who is in you is greater than the one who is in the world" (1 John 4:4). Hallelujah!

Minister the way Jesus did when there is a clear case of somebody being possessed. Bind the strong man, take authority over the demons, and command them to release the person in the name of Jesus. Sometimes, as in Jesus' ministry, the demons will want to be noisy and violent. Follow Jesus' example: command them to be silent. There are no formulas to give you, for you are called to exercise the authority you have. Jesus spoke to the demons sternly; He was not going to stand for any nonsense.

> *You do not need to fear evil spirits.*
> *As a believer, you have power and authority over them.*
> *Do not try to minister in ways you do not properly understand.*
> *But recognize the authority you have as a believer.*

And these signs will accompany those who believe: In my name they will drive out demons" (Mark 16:17).

44

MINISTERING DELIVERANCE

People who want a quiet church life don't want much to do with the kind of ministry Jesus exercised! When He ministered, things happened! Sometimes I cannot help wondering how many churches would want Jesus to minister at their services today. Wherever He is present in the power of the Spirit, He exposes need so that it may be dealt with.

BELIEVE THAT YOU HAVE THE VICTORY

Sometimes at the end of a meeting, people will ask me to pray with someone who is demon-possessed. Usually, a group of well-meaning Christians are standing around the person praying in tongues while the manifestations of the demonic presence are continuing. That is not the way to exercise deliverance. People may be praying but not necessarily believing they have the victory.

The one who speaks in a tongue speaks to God. In this situation, it is the demon who needs to be addressed, and often he is enjoying all the attention he is receiving and the commotion he is causing. The Lord has taught me a very simple but profound truth about deliverance: expect a battle and you will have a battle; expect victory and you will have victory.

In deliverance, we are not initially praying for the person but commanding the demons to leave the person. Satan, if he has possessed someone with one of his demons, does not want to give up. *People can use the right words, but they don't necessarily believe that they have the victory.* It is a question not of using pious language but of exercising authority. Sometimes I might simply say, "Stop that noise. Every demon, you are to leave immediately in the name of Jesus." Then to the person I say, "In the name of Jesus you are set free. Now get up and give thanks to God." Immediately, there is peace, and the person is able to respond because a Christian proclaimed victory. It is a question not of praying long prayers but of *speaking the word of authority in the name of Jesus.*

This is the authority given to every believer. Don't be afraid of the noise, and don't let your faith be in the manifestation taking place before you. The devil loves attention. Certainly, don't allow such things to frighten you. Remember, He who is in you is greater than he who is in the world, and your faith overcomes every spirit opposed to Christ.

Do not seek to exercise such ministry without the proper authority from the church fellowship of which you are a part. This is not a ministry for novices; you need to understand what you are doing.

BEWARE OF DECEPTION

Normally, the devil likes to work unnoticed, manipulating people's lives for his evil purposes. Some Christians imagine they are possessed and ask for deliverance. I cannot remember a single incident when someone asking for deliverance was actually possessed by a demon. Parents have sought deliverance for their children, and that is a different matter. The possessed person may be conscious of needing to be set free, but the demons warn and keep her from going near anyone who would exercise authority over them. Those who seek ministry are more likely to be oppressed rather than possessed.

The devil's business is deception. He is the father of lies. He wants Christians to believe that they can exercise authority over demons only in certain circumstances. Two common fallacies are widespread today. One is that demons have to be named before they can be commanded to leave a person. There is no evidence for this in the New Testament. Jesus did not name all the demons He cast out of Legion. Like Jesus, you are given authority over *all* the works of Satan. The demons are lying if they suggest they have to leave only if named. They have to go because you command them in the name of Jesus.

The second fallacy follows from the first, that you should converse with the demons to discover who they are. It does not matter who they are if you are commanding all of them to go in the name of Jesus. The incident with Legion is usually quoted as the scriptural authority for this practice. But Jesus addressed His question "Who are you?" to the man. The demons replied and begged Jesus to allow them to go into the pigs, who were subsequently drowned.

This episode demonstrates the destructive nature of Satan's activities. When demons possess people, it is to create hatred, violence, sadism, filth, and everything opposed to God's love, both in the possessed people and in others around them. Some have become so familiar with a demonic presence within them that they do not want to be set free. The demons have become so familiar to them that they are afraid of losing them; they fear an essential part of their personalities would be lost if the demons were to leave. In such cases, it is necessary to bring such persons to a point where they want to be delivered and are prepared to renounce Satan and all his works. They can then be delivered.

HEALING ALSO NEEDED

It is not enough to see people rid of the evil presence; *they need to commit their lives to Jesus and to be filled with the Holy Spirit.* Then they will be full of God's love, power, peace, and joy instead of all the negative influences that previously gripped their lives.

Often you will need to follow deliverance with a considerable amount of healing and certainly with building up the person in God's Word. Demonic forces can cause considerable emotional destruction and pain. Many possessed people have lived in an alien culture during the years when possessed, and they need to be brought into a Christian environment where they can be helped and encouraged. The drug culture, alcoholism, transcendental meditation, spiritualism, and the occult provide ample opportunities for demonic spirits to possess people and to influence their lives in horrendous ways. The wounds left by years of abuse need to be healed; the people need to be built up in faith and able to withstand future attacks of the enemy.

The warning Jesus gave should be heeded:

> When an evil spirit comes out of a man, it goes through arid places seeking rest and does not find it. Then it says, "I will return to the house I left." When it arrives, it finds the house swept clean and put in order. Then it goes and takes seven other spirits more wicked than itself, and they go in and live there. And the final condition of that man is worse than the first (Luke 11:24–26).

The clean house needs to be filled with the new life of Jesus, with the power of the Holy Spirit, so that the released people can exercise authority over all the enemy's activities.

In some cases, complete deliverance happens over a period of time as more demonic activity is uncovered and people are led to a personal faith in Jesus.

Submission to His authority means people will no longer submit to the demons who have been influencing them; instead they would be glad to be rid of them.

Expect victory when you confront the enemy.
He will flee from you.
Do not allow yourself to be deceived.
Care with love and healing for those who have been delivered.

And having disarmed the powers and authorities, he made a public spectacle of them, triumphing over them by the cross (Col. 2:15).

45

FREEDOM FOR THE OPPRESSED

Christians, those who are truly born again, are possessed by the Holy Spirit, not by demonic forces. This, however, does not mean there can be no demonic activity in their lives. Sickness is of the devil, and Christians can become sick. Sin delights the devil, and Christians yield to temptation sometimes. Some fall away from faith for a time, becoming involved in all kinds of ungodly activity, and they thus make themselves vulnerable to the enemy.

Satan will not give up his attacks on Christians, obedient or disobedient. If he cannot possess a person, he will attempt to oppress her. Possession means that a demon invades a person's body and manifests his presence through that person. Oppression is attack from without rather than within. It feels as if you are in a cage or prison and need to be set free or as if a great cloud of heaviness has descended on you, and you find it extremely difficult to praise God or to pray.

OPPRESSION THROUGH SIN

Oppression can be the Christian's fault. Through some sin or disobedience, he may have given the enemy opportunity to make him feel truly condemned and utterly useless to God.

He may feel unable to break the power of some particular temptation because he has yielded to it so often.

Oppression also occurs when the enemy is trying to hinder particular individuals, especially in the work of the kingdom. Paul knew plenty of this kind of oppression in his ministry: "We are hard pressed on every side, but not crushed; perplexed, but not in despair; persecuted, but not abandoned; struck down, but not destroyed" (2 Cor. 4:8–9).

Such oppression may come directly or through Satan's use of others to oppose God's children. He can even pit Christian against Christian, causing great damage to the work of the gospel. Paul reminds us, "For our struggle is not against flesh and blood, but against the rulers, against the authorities, against the powers of this dark world and against the spiritual forces of evil in the heavenly realms" (Eph. 6:12).

It is easy for a Christian to blame his problem on the devil when the cause may lie within himself. He may even say he is possessed and therefore unable to do anything about the matter. He will be set free from his problem, he maintains, only if he has deliverance ministry. For example, someone may say, "I believe I have a spirit of lust in me. Will you please pray for me to be delivered?" This person may experience constant temptation to lust to which he sometimes yields. He gives in to the temptation because he wants to, and that exacerbates the problem. But this does not mean he is possessed by a demon of lust.

COOPERATION OF THE BELIEVER

The problem for this believer is not one of possession but one of oppression. The devil can keep putting temptations of lust before him because he knows this Christian's willingness to yield although he knows to do so is sinful. The Christian needs to repent, turning away from the sin, recognizing he has died to sin, and consecrating himself afresh to the Lord. He can take the shield of faith against every attack of the enemy. He can live in the truth that he is a new creation set free by Jesus. He can decide to walk in righteousness. He can take the sword of the Spirit to every attack of the enemy, proclaiming that as a believer he has authority over all the powers of the devil.

We use lust here as an obvious example. The same principle is true of any area of sin.

Whereas the one who is possessed cannot set himself free, the one who is oppressed can—if that is what she wants and is prepared to do. She will need to appreciate that she has been listening to the devil's lies and must turn back to the words of truth. She may need help and encouragement to do this. And she will be encouraged by others standing with her in faith and in prayer against the enemy who has taken advantage of her weakness.

Whereas the one who is possessed finds it difficult to cooperate, the one who is oppressed must cooperate. The Christian must understand that he does not have to allow the enemy to put him into a spiritual prison. Prayer will set him free, but he needs to learn how to resist the enemy's attempts to bring him back into bondage. He needs to believe the positive truths of God's Word instead of the negative lies that come from the devil. Heed Paul's words:

Count yourselves dead to sin but alive to God in Christ Jesus. Therefore do not let sin reign in your mortal body so that you obey its evil desires. Do not offer the parts of your body to sin, as instruments of wickedness, but rather offer yourselves to God, as those who have been brought from death to life; and offer the parts of your body to him as instruments of righteousness. For sin shall not be your master, because you are not under law, but under grace (Rom. 6:11–14).

NEGATIVE DEPRESSION

Some forms of depression are oppression. The enemy feeds the person one negative thought about himself. That negative is received and so is followed by another and then another, until he becomes so negative he feels unable to be positive. He has believed the enemy's lies and now seems powerless to oppose him. The person needs to be delivered not from possession but from oppression. Others can take authority over the enemy and break his hold in the name of Jesus.

When freed, the Christian needs to be taught how to withstand the enemy's attacks by using the shield of faith so that he does not allow himself to be oppressed in the same way again.

OPPRESSION THROUGH SICKNESS

Sometimes a person is oppressed by sickness. Perhaps she has had a particular illness for so long she feels incapable of ever imagining herself to be well or of exercising faith for her healing. Again, others can open the door of the cage or prison for her, but she will need to walk out of it and not return.

Whereas the cooperation of the possessed person is negligible or seriously limited, for the oppressed person it is essential. Otherwise, prayer with her will have only a limited effect, and she will rapidly return to her oppressed state. This is what happens time and again to those who live by their feelings or emotions. They have moments of faith when all seems to be going well, only to drop back into the depths of despair with alarming regularity.

Those who pray with them can exercise faith for them; but they need to be strengthened in their own walk of faith.

OCCULT INFLUENCE

However, other forms of oppression may not be the direct responsibility of the person. Satanic curses are placed upon some individuals and families and can affect those families for several generations. When that is the case, similar problems occur in various members of the family, perhaps suicide or depression, perhaps violence or a particular sickness.

The power of Jesus is able to break the influence of any curse to set individuals or even families free.

Contact with forms of spiritism and the occult can similarly lead to oppression. There may be a medium in the family, or perhaps spiritualists have invoked demonic powers (often unwittingly) in their prayers for an individual. Even if the person concerned has not participated in such activities, he can come under the influence of others around him who have been involved.

Oppression can take the form of emotional bondage or even physical sickness that has its origin in such occult activity. When there is an unresolved problem in a person's experience, it is wise to inquire about any occult influence. The person can then renounce this influence and break the oppression in the name of Jesus and by the power of His blood. He can then deal with the emotional need or physical condition.

WRONG THINKING

Christians can allow wrong spirits to affect their thinking, their attitudes, and their judgments. Criticism is a good example. Within a fellowship someone may be critical of another person and pass on some untrue lie about that person. If others receive that falsehood (without even checking to see if it is correct), they place themselves under the same lies and are likely to pass them on to others. In a short time, this wrong spirit can affect many people. They grow increasingly critical and judgmental without knowing why. This process causes divisions and considerable hurts among God's people.

The answer is to confess the sin and command this wrong spirit to depart so that it is unable to influence the fellowship any further.

ADDRESS THE ENEMY

Satan uses demons to oppress as well as possess. He can be bound and the demons commanded to release their oppressive hold. Often when Christians experience a time of great turmoil and conflict, they pray and agonize, "Lord, help me. Lord, help me. Lord, set me free from this." If they are dealing with the enemy, they also need to address Satan in the name of Jesus. This is particularly true when the enemy is trying to oppress by hindering the work of the kingdom. All believers need to exercise their authority to prevent themselves from being oppressed and to rebuke the enemy because Satan will try to oppress every child of God. All experience times of intense opposition, of heaviness or pressure, when it seems extremely difficult to walk in the Spirit, and it is necessary to recognize the source of what is happening and come against the devil's activity using the power and authority given them in the name of Jesus.

The enemy will use spirits of unbelief to try to oppose your walk of faith, especially for healing. He does not want you healed, even though God does. *Tell Satan to depart. You are going to listen not to the voice of demons but to the Word of God.*

Be aware of the deviousness of the enemy. Don't waste your sympathy on him. *Tell him and all his oppressive powers to go in the name of Jesus. You are being led in God's triumphant procession. Because you are living in the victory of Jesus, you are going to see victory over the powers of darkness.* You don't have to be afraid; you live in the power and victory of the Lord.

God said, "I have indeed seen the oppression of my people in Egypt. I have heard their groaning and have come down to set them free" (Acts 7:34). *He has already come in an even more wonderful way in His Son, Jesus, to break every power of oppression.*

> *You do not have to stand any nonsense with demons. You have authority over them in the name of Jesus. Walk in the glorious liberty of the children of God.*

For you died, and your life is now hidden with Christ in God (Col. 3:3).

Part Eight

FAILURE

46

FAILURE THROUGH ERROR

Even though through the Cross God has made provision for the complete healing of His children in spirit, soul, and body, it is evident that believers do not manifest such wholeness. Even though healings and miracles are commonplace where there is genuine faith in Jesus to intervene supernaturally to meet needs, it is obvious that not all who pray or receive ministry manifest healing. Even though God desires to heal all, apparently not all are healed. Why?

Some reasons have become clear already. We must beware of concentrating on reasons for not being healed instead of placing our attention on Jesus, who wants to give us faith for healing. However, we need to face failure honestly and understand the reasons for it.

It would be wrong to place the burden of failure entirely on the sick person. Often there is corporate unbelief, a lack of power in the body of Christ, or a lack of authority in those who minister. Sometimes the failure is both personal and corporate.

There are times when I am deeply conscious of my failure—sometimes failure to appropriate healing for myself but more often my inability to bring healing to others, frequently in a chronic condition. Recognition of this failure spurs me on to seek the Lord for more faith and authority in my ministry.

UNBELIEF

From all we have seen of Jesus' teaching and His attitude toward healing, it must be said that unbelief is the most widespread cause of failure. When the disciples asked why they had been unable to heal the boy with epilepsy, Jesus answered, "Because you have so little faith" (Matt. 17:20). They believed in Jesus Himself, but they did not believe they had the authority to heal in that particular situation.

There are many today who believe in Jesus and have a definite love and devotion for Him. That does not necessarily mean that they have faith for their healing.

At Nazareth, Jesus was astonished at the unbelief of those who knew Him: "He could not do any miracles there, except lay his hands on a few sick people and heal them. And he was amazed at their lack of faith" (Mark 6:5–6).

By contrast, Jesus says that nothing is impossible for those with faith and "anyone who has faith in me will do what I have been doing" (John 14:12).

We see then that unbelief in the sick person or in those surrounding him or ministering can affect the outcome. Unbelief prevents a person from receiving what God is willing to give.

The unbelief of the church locally or nationally has serious consequences. The double-mindedness of the church toward healing makes it unstable and unable to receive from God. Jesus, the apostles, and the early church were single-minded about the matter, and so *all* who turned to the Lord for healing were healed.

When the church today is cleansed of this double-mindedness, we shall see far more healings. Those who minister healing do so in a general climate of unbelief, which is hardly helpful.

IGNORANCE

Where there is no faith for healing and there is little authority in those who preach and teach, there will be a sad lack of people's needs being met. If healing is both taught and practiced, there will be healings. Where the subject is either avoided or spoken against, there will be a marked absence of healing. People are kept in ignorance of God's purpose, so they do not have any expectation that God will meet them in their need.

I constantly come across Christians for whom it is a new revelation that Jesus heals today. Their ignorance, often not of their own making, has kept them in bondage to disease. What a great responsibility there is on all preachers to proclaim the *whole* counsel of God. Paul said, "I have not hesitated to preach anything that would be helpful to you" (Acts 20:20). And he added, "For I have not hesitated to proclaim to you the whole will of God" (v. 27).

Ignorance of the Word leads to ignorance of God's purposes. It is only when people know His will that they can exercise faith.

WRONG TEACHING

Ignorance of God's healing purposes means that people will not look to the Lord with faith for their healing. *Wrong teaching can prevent other Christians from receiving their healing.*

Some mistakenly say that healing was only for the apostolic age and should not take place today. The age of miracles has passed, they suggest. Others claim it is not God's purpose to heal physically and that Jesus did not atone for physical sickness on the cross.

Some claim that God is glorified if a person remains sick,

so they teach that sickness should be accepted as His will for the believer.

When Christians are continuously subjected to such mistaken teaching, it is understandable that they find it difficult to shake off the shackles of the past when the truth is revealed to them that God does heal today. Some Christians cannot cope with this information. I have heard of people being asked to leave churches because they have been healed, sometimes of incurable diseases. Other members of these fellowships have been unwilling to change their thinking or adjust their mistaken theology. Such is the fruit of religious prejudice!

Personal opinions stand in the way of faith. Your opinions or ideas carry no weight with God, but He watches over His Word to perform it.

"ALL HEALING HAS TO BE INSTANTANEOUS"

The misconception that healing is always immediate leads many to think that unless they receive a miracle during the time of their prayer and ministry, it is not God's purpose to heal at that time. All healing has to happen instantaneously or not at all, they feel. To substantiate this position, people point to Jesus' ministry and say that everyone He prayed for was healed immediately.

Nowhere does Jesus teach us that all answers to prayer will be instantaneous. We enjoy such occasions, but we learn that often we have to inherit God's promises like Abraham—by faith with patience: "Whatever you ask in prayer, believe that you have received it, and it will be yours" (Mark 11:24).

Healings begin at certain moments of faith, but sometimes they take time to be fully accomplished. The danger is that those who hold to this view of instantaneous healing look to the symptoms after the prayer rather than to God's words of promise.

Counteract these negatives with the positive truth.

> *God has given you faith—put it in His Word.*
> *Feed on His Word so that you will not be ignorant of His*
> *purposes.*
> *Counteract wrong teaching and mistaken ideas by*
> *submitting your thinking to God's thinking—through*
> *His Word.*

Trust in the LORD with all your heart and lean not on your own understanding (Prov. 3:5).

47

SOME MISTAKEN IDEAS

It is never helpful to our faith to argue against God's Word. Faith comes from hearing and receiving His Word. It is good to be rid of the negative so that we can concentrate on the positive and allow God to speak faith to our hearts, thus enabling us to receive the healing He wants to give.

"GOD SENDS SICKNESS FOR OUR GOOD"

Many people testify that God has used sickness for good in their lives. Not only can it be a refining instrument in the life of the sick person, but also the way in which sickness is borne by Christians can be a great witness to those who are not believers. However, this does not mean that sickness is God's best purpose. He is the Redeemer who is able to turn any situation of evil and use it for His good. *Better to allow Him to refine you in health than in sickness.*

His best purpose is that you are never sick. If you are sick, His next best purpose is to heal you. If for some reason the healing does not take place immediately, He will certainly use that situation for good.

Jesus never refused anyone who came to Him for healing. Never did He send people away, telling them that sickness was God's will for them, that He wanted them ill, or that they were being disciplined through the sickness for their own good. *He simply healed them, demonstrating that healing was His Father's will.*

Jesus clearly saw sickness as Satan's work, and He came to destroy all the works of the devil. Paul says that "in all things God works for the good of those who love him, who have been called according to his purpose" (Rom. 8:28). In sickness He is willing to work for *your* good. The difficulties and sicknesses we encounter can be used creatively and positively by God. When Christians search their hearts and seek to hear what God is saying to them in times of sickness, He is able to use these times creatively in their lives. When Christians feel bitter and resentful toward God for allowing them to be sick, their independence, rebellion, disobedience, and anger toward God are revealed. The sickness does not create these attitudes; it exposes what is in the heart already.

There needs to be repentance of these wrong heart attitudes before people are able to receive the healing God wants to give them. Refusing to repent is akin to condemning oneself to death—not only of sickness but of a heart full of bitter and resentful anger toward the Lord.

God is able to redeem the situation and use the sickness creatively, but this does not make it His purpose for His child. Many have acknowledged that sickness has given them time to pause, think, seek God, pray, and hear Him speak into their lives in ways they had not previously heard. Often this is because they have been racing around in such a fever of overactivity, it seems God has had to lay them low in order to get their attention. If this is the case, it is certainly not God's best will. He does not want us to be so overactive and busy that we do not allow time to attend to what He is saying.

Sometimes we hear clearly what God is asking of us, but we do not pay heed to His words. *During times of sickness, some have faced more fully and completely God's will for their lives and the claims He has been making upon them as their Lord.* But God does not beat His children into submission through sickness. If that were true, as soon as they have responded obediently to Him, they could rightly expect the sickness to be removed immediately. He wants a free response of love from the heart.

"GOD IS GLORIFIED IN SICKNESS"

It is not right for Christians to rejoice in their sickness and imagine that illness is God's best purpose for them or that He is glorified in sickness. If it is possible for God to be glorified in illness, Jesus deprived Him of glory by healing *all* who came to Him. He never refused to heal people, saying He would leave them in the sickness that His Father might be glorified in their lives.

God wants His children to be in good health, able to be faithful witnesses to His love and power. It is inconceivable to think of Jesus as sick, and the clear command of Scripture is that we are to walk as Jesus did. This is God's purpose, His best intention for all His children.

When any of God's children submit to sickness, it may be because they find it easier to seek His will and remain in a position of holiness because of their physical weakness. This is hardly God's best purpose, for although in sickness people may be saved from the temptations of the world around them, the Lord calls them to be fruitful and faithful witnesses in the world.

Some Christians do not want to be healed because they enjoy the attention, the sympathy, and even the self-pity they experience during times of illness. If God were to remove the sickness, they would probably become sick again to receive once more the attention they want from others. So they justify their sickness as being the will of God and claim it is not His purpose to heal them.

Jesus says that His Father is glorified when we bear much fruit, not when we are sick. He came to do His Father's will, and He accomplished that by meeting people's needs, not telling them to suffer as God's purpose for His children.

"GOD IS TEACHING ME IN SICKNESS"

We have seen that God is able to redeem every situation in our lives. He can use everything creatively. Of course, He can teach us in sickness. *But He teaches us also in health. And He much prefers to teach us in health, not in sickness.* The fact that a person is learning spiritual lessons while ill does not justify the sickness or mean that illness is God's best purpose for His child.

One of the lessons many have to learn in times of sickness is that they do not believe God's love and grace are such that He wills to heal them. If you believe God has a lesson to teach you in your sickness, hurry up and learn it so that you can receive your healing!

"WE ALL HAVE TO DIE SOME TIME"

What about death? There is no fear in death for a Christian. It is not a defeat but the gateway to the greatest victory of all, for those who believe in Jesus will experience resurrection and will enjoy His eternal glory.

Some say Christians want it both ways, healing in this life and victorious resurrection if they die. We can triumphantly proclaim that we do have the best of both worlds. God's purpose is to heal us in this life, and He will raise us into His glorious kingdom beyond this life. Hallelujah!

Healing is not a means of escaping death; the time for us all to die will inevitably come. This does not mean God wants you to die prematurely, before your life has run its full course. Neither does it indicate that God desires you to die from a long, protracted, and painful sickness.

Death is not to be an escape from life. Paul says it is far better to go to be with the Lord—but not before fulfilling His purpose here on earth.

Satan loves to encourage a fear of death. Often sickness is attended by a spirit of death over which Christians need to take authority in the name of Jesus. Such spirits cause many deaths that are medically inexplicable, either because the cause of death cannot be determined or because people fail to respond to treatment in the expected way.

So because someone seems to be at the point of death and is beyond medical help, it does not mean that this is necessarily God's appointed hour of death for that person. It is too easy to say, "The Lord took him," when a Christian dies, his body ravaged by disease.

Certainly, the Lord has the ultimate victory in the believer's resurrection. But if He wants to take one of His children to glory, He does not have to resort to painful sickness to do so.

Many have been healed when on the very point of death, and some have been brought back to life when they have died. Never forget that the devil is the thief who steals, kills, and destroys. It is Jesus who came to give life.

There comes the right time for every believer to be with the Lord. I have known older people to be healed and delivered from pain before peacefully going to their Savior soon afterward.

There are other occasions when the Lord makes clear that a person is going to die of a sickness. Although that may not be His desire, that is what is going to happen.

And there are times when the Spirit tells those praying to release the sick person to Him. We need have no fear in doing that for

> the righteous are taken away
> to be spared from evil.
> Those who walk uprightly
> enter into peace;
> they find rest as they lie in death (Isa. 57:1–2).

God sends healing, not sickness, for your good.
God is glorified in healing, not in sickness.
God wants to teach you in health, rather than in sickness.
God wants to take you to His glory at His appointed time. He does not want the thief to snatch your life from you.

Dear friend, I pray that you may enjoy good health and that all may go well with you, even as your soul is getting along well (3 John 2).

48

MORE MISTAKEN
IDEAS

"GOD CALLS US TO SUFFER FOR HIM"

Christians are called to suffer for the sake of the gospel, but they are not called by God to sickness and disease. There is a clear distinction in Scripture between suffering and sickness. Some may have to suffer persecution and painful death, even with torture, because of their Christian witness. That can be the cost of remaining faithful to the Lord in a sick and fallen world.

These things may be inevitable in the world in which we live, and they are certainly within the permissive will of God. He allows these things to happen, but that does not mean that He *desires* them to happen. *Suffering for the sake of the gospel has creative and positive results*. Much useless suffering and sickness in the world appear to have no positive and fruitful effects for the kingdom of God.

Christian discipleship can be costly. Obedience to God's will can be demanding. But nowhere does Jesus call His followers to come and be sick for Him!

"THIS IS THE CROSS I HAVE TO CARRY"

If you are carrying sickness as your cross, you are carrying the wrong cross. Jesus bore your infirmities on His cross so that you could be relieved of them and spared from carrying them. The cross He calls you to carry is that of self-denial, of what you willingly choose to take up day by day to follow Him: "If anyone would come after me, he must deny himself and take up his cross daily and follow me. For whoever wants to save his life will lose it, but whoever loses his life for me will save it" (Luke 9:23–24).

These words are addressed to *anyone* who would be a follower of Jesus. Every disciple is called to self-denial but not to sickness. The Greek word translated "life" can also be translated "soul" and does not refer to the physical body.

Be sure that you are carrying the right cross, that you choose each day to walk the path of faith and loving obedience. Do not carry the sickness that the enemy or fear or your own sin has inflicted upon you and then imagine that it is the cross you carry for Christ.

"NOT EVERYBODY IS HEALED"

Many people use this statement to excuse themselves from actively believing God for their own healing. We have seen that on the cross God has made provision for the healing of all His people. All are healed on the cross, but not all receive their healing. One of the major reasons for that is unbelief, not only the unbelief of the individual but also the corporate unbelief of the church.

"Not everybody is healed" is true when a doctor heals. But that does not mean she will give up practicing medicine. All the time she is seeking to be more proficient and knowledge-able in her particular field of expertise.

Far from being deterred by apparent failure, Christians should be spurred on by their inability to minister the Lord's healing power in some situations. They should want to increase in faith, power, and authority that God may be glorified more fully in the healing of His people.

As Christians, we are involved in a spiritual fight against the powers of darkness, confident of the victory we have in the Lord Jesus Christ. Because of our unbelief and lack of perfection, we do not always see the victory in our battle against disease. That victory is God's purpose, and it was perfectly manifested in the ministry of Jesus. He healed *all* who came to Him. That is the ideal at which we are to aim. It was certainly fulfilled at times in the apostolic church, for we read in the book of Acts that the apostles also healed all who came to them.

God wants to increase our faith in His desire and willingness to heal and our knowledge of how we can avail ourselves of His healing resources. Then we will see God glorified in the healing of many more people, which will be in itself a witness to the world that the kingdom of God is present not only in talk but also in power.

"GOD SENDS SICKNESS AS A PUNISHMENT FOR SIN"

In the Old Testament, God allowed sickness to come upon His people during times when they were disobedient. And so some have maintained that we should regard sickness as the Lord's chastisement.

But Jesus bore the punishment of our sins on the cross so that we need not suffer the punishment we deserve. Yet some have such a negative view of sickness that they truly believe this to be God's way of punishing them. If they believe that, they are incapable of looking to Him with faith, expecting Him to heal.

If sickness is a punishment for sin, there is no need for further punishment as soon as forgiveness is received. *This means that God would have to remove it as soon as there was repentance on the part of the believer.* Otherwise He would not be just and righteous.

Some sicknesses are a direct consequence of sin, although Jesus makes it clear that is not the case with all illness. If the sickness is the consequence of sin, the sickness should disappear as soon as there is forgiveness.

When a man blind from birth was brought to Jesus, He was asked whether the blindness was the result of the man's own sin or that of his parents. Jesus answered, "Neither this man nor his parents sinned . . . but this happened so that the work of God might be displayed in his life. As long as it is day, we must do the work of him who sent me" (John 9:3–4). Jesus then did the work of God by restoring the man's sight. Notice that Jesus said, "We must do the work of him who sent me." That healing work is shared by all who believe in Him.

"GOD HAS PERMITTED ME TO BE SICK, SO I MUST ACCEPT IT"

Sickness is part of the *permissive* will of God. He allows His children to be sick, just as He allows us to sin—although He desires neither sickness nor sin for us. If we step outside the holy covenant He has made with us as our Father, we make ourselves vulnerable to the enemy's attacks. Jesus regards sickness as coming from the devil. But the devil is allowed to operate only under God's permissive will. That means Satan is allowed to go only where God gives him leave to go. It is therefore thought by some that sickness can occur only when God gives Satan leave to inflict one of His children with sickness.

On the other hand, we have to acknowledge that Satan is our adversary, and he continually tries to upset us and prevent us from doing God's will. Sickness is one of the ways in which he tries to cut us down in the prime of life and prevent us from fulfilling Spirit-anointed ministries. This is not God's will. It may be that the enemy is able to take advantage of some impediment or weakness in us that allows him to have a foothold of sickness in our lives.

Whenever a Christian is ill, it is obviously important not only for him to turn immediately to the Lord to be healed but also for him to seek to hear from God what He is saying in this situation, especially if the healing does not begin to manifest itself immediately.

If you accept your sickness, you will find it virtually impossible to receive your healing. You are called to fight against sickness, not yield to it.

Is there a physical need that has been perplexing you for some time? Have you sought the Lord and asked Him what He is saying to you in this situation? If so, have you responded to what it is that He has said to you? Has He pointed out things that need amending in your life? Perhaps there has been some relationship that needs to be put right, or there is some area of disobedience about which God is wanting to deal with you. Do you feel bitter or angry toward Him for allowing your sickness?

If any of these things is true for you, do business with the Lord now and let Him deal with these matters; then there will be no impediment to your receiving the healing that He wants to pour into your life.

Remember, God does not *want* you to be sick. He wants you to be walking around in faithful and loving obedience to His will and purpose.

> *God calls you to suffer for the gospel; He does not call*
> *you to sickness.*
> *God calls you to carry the cross of self-denial, not*
> *sickness.*
> *God wants to heal you in spirit, soul, and body.*
> *God does not want to punish you; He has provided for*
> *your forgiveness.*
> *God does not want you to accept sickness but wants you*
> *to accept the provision of His healing.*

The LORD is faithful to all his promises and loving toward
all he has made (Ps. 145:13).

49

FAILURE THROUGH EXCUSES

PAUL'S THORN

The attitude of some people is to look for reasons why they
should not be healed rather than believe the revelation of
God's Word that He has already done on the cross all that is
necessary for our total healing. To justify their unbelief, they
turn to Scripture to find possible exceptions to the truth that
God wants to heal all. By far the most common way of doing
this is to point to Paul's thorn in the flesh.

It is amazing how many people, including preachers, totally misinterpret this passage of the Bible. Nowhere does Paul suggest that this thorn is a sickness or disease. He describes this thorn as "a messenger of Satan," sent to torment him (2 Cor. 12:7). The word translated as "messenger" appears 188 times in the New Testament. On 181 occasions, the Greek word is translated "angel"; on the other 7, "messenger" is used. On all occasions, it refers to a person, never to an object or a disease.

In modern colloquial English, we refer to a problem person as being a pain in the neck or a thorn in my side. Elsewhere in the Bible the latter phrase is used to describe the enemies of God's people: "But if you do not drive out the inhabitants of the land, those you allow to remain will become barbs in your eyes and thorns in your sides. They will give you trouble in the land where you will live" (Num. 33:55).

It seems, therefore, that Paul was praying to God about someone who was opposing his work of proclaiming the gospel. We know from other references, including several in this same epistle, that Paul was constantly harassed by such opposition. Although he outlines many hardships he faced, *nowhere does he include sickness among them.*

The Lord told Paul, "My grace is sufficient for you, for my power is made perfect in weakness" (2 Cor. 12:9). It is common for a preacher to feel weak in the face of constant opposition; yet God's grace enables him to persevere faithfully, recognizing that the awareness of his own weakness creates greater dependence on the Lord.

And so Paul continues, "Therefore I will boast all the more gladly about my weaknesses, so that Christ's power may rest on me. That is why, for Christ's sake, I delight in weaknesses, in insults, in hardships, in persecutions, in difficulties. For when I am weak, then I am strong" (vv. 9–10). *He does not include diseases in his list.* In the previous chapter (11:23–30), he lists the kind of hardships he faced, again with *no mention of sickness.*

Even if Paul's thorn was a sickness, which clearly it was not, it would be necessary to weigh that one verse of Scripture against all the other evidence of God's will to heal contained in the Bible. Certainly, Paul would not have delighted in sickness when he was such a powerful instrument of God's healing.

It is sad that so many should have clung to this one episode in an attempt to prove that it is not always God's purpose to heal instead of clinging to all the other verses of Scripture demonstrating clearly that it is His desire to heal.

LOOKING AT OTHERS' EXPERIENCES

Again in attempting to justify a failure to receive healing or believe in God's will to heal, some people point to other notable Christian men and women who have either died of disease or remained with disabilities.

We have seen how dangerous it is to base doctrine on experience rather than on God's Word. Unless involved personally in a particular case, it is usually impossible to say why a person did not, or does not, receive healing. *What cannot be questioned is God's willingness to heal and the provision He has already made for that purpose to be fulfilled.*

The fact that someone else does not appear to receive healing is no justification to doubt God's will in your life.

Sometimes I have a physical need that persists for some time while I see hundreds or thousands of others healed. That does not mean God wants to leave me out of the blessing. He wants me to appropriate my healing in Jesus' name.

So avoid the temptation to look at others' experiences. Look to the Lord and His Word, and enter into the inheritance that is yours.

> *Do not look for excuses.*
> *Do not look at others' experiences.*
> *Look to Jesus.*
> *Look to His Word and His promises.*

Let us draw near to God with a sincere heart in full assurance of faith (Heb. 10:22).

50

FAILURE THROUGH LACK

LACK OF POWER

Jesus said, "But you will receive power when the Holy Spirit comes on you" (Acts 1:8). How can we heal in Jesus' name without the power of the Spirit being released in our lives and ministries?

Jesus Himself experienced a baptism in the Holy Spirit at the outset of His preaching and healing ministry. He was already conceived of the Holy Spirit; the Spirit already lived in Him. Yet He received the endowment of power to commission Him for His ministry.

To receive baptism in the Holy Spirit does not deny the indwelling power of the Holy Spirit in the new birth. It means that the believer recognizes that there needs to be a release of power in the life and ministry.

Those who claim to have received such power at conversion usually do not demonstrate much evidence of that in healing *whereas those who have a definite experience of baptism in the Spirit receive faith for God to heal.*

For this reason I will normally lead people to receive such a baptism in the Holy Spirit before praying for them to be healed. The Spirit will increase their faith in the Word, in His willingness to heal, and in His personal love for them. The work of the Spirit is intensified in their lives so that they are able to receive their healing more easily.

If you have not been baptized in the Holy Spirit, know that God intends this for you and for every believer. Ask Him to fulfill this promise in your life, knowing that it is His purpose to give it to you.

LACK OF SPIRITUAL GIFTS

Baptism in the Holy Spirit releases the gifts of the Spirit in a person's experience. These gifts are an essential part of the resources necessary for those who want to minister healing.

Healing has to do with the supernatural power of God at work in the lives of His children. These are the supernatural gifts that give us supernatural understanding and ability to minister to those in need. It would seem foolish to ignore the very things that God has made available so that our ministries might be fruitful.

At times words of wisdom and knowledge are needed. The gifts of healings are gifts of the Spirit—as are miracles and the ability to distinguish between spirits, to know whether something is from God, a man or woman, or the devil. A word of prophecy can open the way to healing. And the ability to speak in a language given by the Spirit is invaluable. When you do not know how to pray with your limited understanding, the Spirit can pray through you whatever needs to be said.

When we recognize the centrality of faith in the healing ministry, we see the importance of the gift of faith. Without these gifts, we are deprived of the tools of our trade as believers.

LACK OF AUTHORITY

Lack of authority follows unbelief. Where there is a lack of faith, there will be a lack of authority. All pastors and elders are supposed to minister the healing power of Jesus to His people. Without faith in God's Word, they will not believe they have authority to heal in His name and to overcome all the enemy's power.

Jesus, the apostles, and others in the New Testament demonstrated that authority needs to be expressed in ministering to people who are sick. The same is true today. People are drawn to services and meetings where individuals of authority are preaching God's Word, for they know healing will attend the preaching. That should be true whenever the gospel is proclaimed, in every congregation or fellowship.

Pastors and elders need to be baptized in the Holy Spirit and experienced in the use of the spiritual gifts if they are going to fulfill effectively God's call on their lives: to bring healing and wholeness of spirit, soul, and body to His people in the name of Jesus.

LACK OF DISCERNMENT

If a disease has a demonic origin, prayer does not meet the need. We must bind the evil spirit and free the person from its influence.

Jesus addressed the demons and commanded them to leave when the illness was the result of such activity. He told the disciples to cast out demons, and He teaches us that in prayer we need to speak to the mountains and command them to move. He commissions us to heal sick persons, not simply pray for them.

When we exercise the authority we have bee
often necessary to speak to the disease and cor
Jesus' name to leave the person. Then it is righ
Lord to heal and to restore every bodily function t

FAILURE TO LISTEN

In every situation, God is speaking to us by the Spirit. The object of prayer is not for us to do all the talking and God all the listening. We need to allow the Lord to speak and to heed what He is saying.

It is important for the person with the illness and those ministering to her to listen to what God is saying. He may well point to another need that has to be resolved before the physical healing can take place. This may involve repenting, forgiving others, or facing some emotional crisis. The Spirit may point to an oppressive bondage in the individual or her family. He will give discernment about how to pray and what to pray.

Insensitivity to the voice of the Spirit seriously limits our capacity to receive from God. To any minister of the gospel, particularly in healing, it is essential to learn to hear the Lord by spending time waiting on Him. Notice how sensitive Jesus was to His Father's voice; He spoke only what His Father gave Him to speak.

> *Be filled with the power of the Holy Spirit.*
> *The gifts of the Spirit are available to you.*
> *As a believer, you have authority to heal in Jesus' name.*
> *God will give you wisdom when you ask for it.*
> *Listen to the voice of the Spirit.*

But you will receive power when the Holy Spirit comes on you (Acts 1:8).

51

PERSONAL FAILURE

UNFORGIVENESS

Unwillingness to forgive someone who has offended the sick person will result in his inability to receive healing. If he does not forgive others, he is not himself forgiven. If unforgiven, he is in no fit state of grace to receive his healing.

It is quite common for the person concerned to refuse to face the pain of a broken relationship, of bitterness, or of hatred that may have been stored up within him for years. The healing will not take place until he does. God, in His love and wisdom, wants the bitterness and the relationship healed, as well as the physical disorder.

UNRIGHTED WRONGS

Just as it is important to forgive others, so it is also important to go to others and ask for their forgiveness when we have wronged them. An unwillingness to do this can hinder God's healing purposes.

Sometimes He asks us to make restitution to people. Failure to obey the Spirit in this can also delay the healing.

DISOBEDIENCE

We cannot expect God to heal if in our lives there are areas of deliberate disobedience to His will. That is tantamount to saying, "Never mind about Your will, Lord; just heal me."

What you say in prayer is said within the context of your relationship with God. If that relationship is strained because of your disobedience, it is unlikely you will have any confidence when praying. It is better to submit to the Lord and His claims on your life so that you may then receive your healing.

One of the causes for a time delay in appropriating healing through the prayer of faith or one of the sacramental acts can be disobedience. When the believer yields to the Lord and turns from her disobedience, the healing immediately takes place without the need of further prayer or ministry.

We cannot fool the Lord. He knows everything about us, and we can hide nothing from Him.

WRONG MOTIVES

God heals not for our pride but for His glory. As we give testimony about healing, it is important not to steal glory from the Lord.

He will heal in evangelistic situations, but we do not ask for healing in such a way as to suggest that it will be a wonderful example to nonbelievers or an encouragement to the local congregation. That can sound like spiritual blackmail. We pray for healing because it is God's will and He is to be glorified in the healing. We want to please Him rather than impress others. We desire to see Him confirming His Word with signs following, not exalting the one who ministers the Word in His name.

UNWILLINGNESS TO GIVE

The scriptural principle Jesus teaches is this: "Give, and it will be given to you. A good measure, pressed down, shaken together and running over, will be poured into your lap. For with the measure you use, it will be measured to you" (Luke 6:38).

If we expect God to give to us, we need to be obedient in our giving to Him and to others according to His Word. A failure to tithe is robbing God. And He wants us to give not begrudgingly but cheerfully: "Each man should give what he has decided in his heart to give, not reluctantly or under compulsion, for God loves a cheerful giver. And God is able to make all grace abound to you, so that in all things at all times, having all that you need, you will abound in every good work" (2 Cor. 9:7–8).

LOOKING AT THE SYMPTOMS

Some people are prepared to believe God only when the symptoms have completely disappeared. That is not faith. If they pray or receive ministry and the symptoms are still obvious, they conclude that the healing has not happened because it is not God's purpose to heal at that time.

We are to bring light against the darkness—not concentrate on the darkness—and have faith in the midst of the problem. Faith operates before the event, not after it!

Faith is faith only when we speak it and act upon it. We need to act out our faith. If we believe we have received when we pray, we will speak of ourselves as healed people, not sick ones. We shall begin to walk in healing, not in sickness. Some receive prayer but continue to languish in bed because they do not obey the prompting of the Spirit to act upon the word of healing they have received. Faith is not merely believing that God has spoken but acting on what He says!

LOOKING AT SELF

It is all too common for believers to look at themselves, conscious of their total unworthiness, and to conclude that

God would not want to heal them. He is the God of grace, who gives freely to those who deserve nothing. If God waited until we deserved to receive from Him, He would give us nothing.

Obviously, it is right to seek His forgiveness. When He forgives, He cleanses us and makes us worthy in His sight and able to receive from Him. *Many do not have faith for healing because they have never believed the graciousness of God in forgiving and accepting them.*

LACK OF PERSEVERANCE

Halfheartedness in prayer is revealed by a lack of perseverance. Even if there is great intensity at first, the lack of real trust in God is demonstrated if the person becomes resigned to the situation, believing the sickness to be God's will for her and that for some reason He does not want to heal her.

When symptoms appear to grow worse instead of better, many give up believing. Sometimes there is an intensification of the symptoms before the healing. Even if they begin to disappear, faith should not be in that experience but in the Lord Himself and in His Word. We receive healing by having faith not in our experience or lack of it but in what Jesus has already accomplished on the cross.

NO PERSONAL REVELATION

The absence of personal revelation is one of the most common causes of failure. A person may believe it is God's will to heal but does not receive revelation of His Word that he has received the healing.

We do not need revelation to know that it is God's purpose to heal; that is clear from the Bible. But the believer needs that moment of personal revelation, of living faith, that enables him to appropriate the healing God wants to give him.

Such revelation comes from a personal encounter with the Lord—through prayer, through the Spirit declaring the words of Scripture to his heart, through a meeting where healing is offered, or through others ministering to him. At some point there is that personal word from God that unlocks the situation.

Knowledge of verses about healing in Scripture is not of itself sufficient. *Knowledge is no substitute for revelation. The Spirit enables the promise to be received as a personal word from God.*

ABUSE OF THE BODY

If we abuse our bodies, we can become sick. If that abuse continues, it is unlikely that healing will result. An obvious example is someone with lung cancer who smokes. The Lord would want to deal with the smoking if the cancer is to be healed. He does not give His healing life that we may continue to abuse our bodies or walk in disobedience.

Some have had a genuine healing from God, but after a few months, the disease recurs. This is inevitable if people have continued in disobedience, for they have given the enemy opportunity.

They may have confessed bitterness and received forgiveness and healing of a particular disease. But if they allow the heart to become bitter and resentful again, it is not surprising if the physical stress symptoms return.

> *Forgive.*
> *Ask others to forgive you when necessary.*
> *Obey the Lord.*
> *Be healed for His glory.*
> *Give, and it will be given to you.*
> *Hear Jesus speak personally to you by the Spirit.*
> *Don't look at your symptoms or yourself; look at Him.*

Let us then approach the throne of grace with confidence, so that we may receive mercy and find grace to help us in our time of need (Heb. 4:16).

||||||||||||||||||||||||||||||||||||||||||||||||||||||||||

Part Nine

THE HEALING
CHURCH

||||||||||||||||||||||||||||||||||||||||||||||||||||||||||

52

IN THE NAME OF JESUS

THE HEALING OF THE MAN WITH
A DISABILITY

Jesus could act on His own faith and authority, and He taught the disciples to do likewise. On many occasions He must have passed the man disabled since birth, who was laid at the gate of the temple every day. Yet Jesus did not heal him. No doubt the disciples also had passed him often. On that particular day when the man asked Peter and John for money,

Peter said, "Look at us!" So the man gave them his attention, expecting to get something from them.

Then Peter said, "Silver or gold I do not have, but what I have I give you. In the name of Jesus Christ of Nazareth, walk." Taking him by the right hand, he helped him up, and instantly the man's feet and ankles became strong. He jumped to his feet and began to walk. Then he went with them into the temple courts, walking and jumping, and praising God (Acts 3:4–8).

It seems that the man expected that he would receive from the apostles, but no doubt he was expecting money, not his healing. The Holy Spirit must have impressed upon Peter and John that they were to heal the man in the name of Jesus.

God had a purpose beyond that of healing the man. It provided the opportunity for Peter and John to preach to a large crowd in the temple courts, for everyone knew the man who was previously disabled, and his healing naturally caused a great stir.

AN EVANGELISTIC OPPORTUNITY

The evangelistic opportunity gave Peter the opening to declare, "By faith in the name of Jesus, this man whom you see and know was made strong. It is Jesus' name and the faith that comes through him that has given this complete healing to him, as you can all see" (Acts 3:16). Faith was certainly in operation—in Peter and John.

What was the result of the incident? Peter and John were arrested; that can be the cost of preaching the gospel. The fruit was that "many who heard the message believed, and the number of men grew to about five thousand" (4:4).

Through two Christians exercising faith, many others were brought to faith. And Peter and John were given the opportunity to testify before the high priest's family, the elders and teachers of the law: "It is by the name of Jesus Christ of Nazareth, whom you crucified but whom God raised from the dead, that this man stands before you healed"(v. 10).

They went on to preach Jesus as the only means of salvation. "But since they could see the man who had been healed standing there with them, there was nothing they could say" (v. 14) to refute the disciples' claims. The leaders had to acknowledge, "Everybody living in Jerusalem knows they have done an outstanding miracle, and we cannot deny it" (v. 16).

THE POWER OF JESUS' NAME

Because of their opposition to Him, the leaders were afraid of the name of Jesus and wanted to stop Peter and John from preaching in His name. *This is the name above every name*, the name in which you have the privilege to pray.

Peter made it clear that it was by faith in the name of Jesus that the man was healed. Has the name of Jesus less power now than then? Certainly not. Jesus is reigning in triumph and power. Faith in His name today will bring the same results—or even greater ones!

Those who suggest God's healing is not for today are suggesting that the name of Jesus is now less powerful. What they lack is faith in that name, to believe Jesus to heal now as He did then.

At an evening meeting during our recent summer camp, I invited people to come forward if they believed the Lord would heal them. I asked them to look straight at me, and I told them to receive the words I spoke as coming from Jesus Himself: "In the name of Jesus receive your healing." "By the stripes of Jesus you are healed."

The power of God was obviously touching people's lives as they received the words. As they received the words in their hearts, they received healing in their bodies.

Among the hundreds who came forward were all the members of a family who had been involved in a traffic accident. All had sustained injuries, but their main concern was for the teenage son who had incurred brain damage.

A few days ago I met the mother. She told me that every member of the family was healed that evening—including the teenage son, who had just been declared fit by the bewildered doctors.

The power of God continued to move that evening, and it ended with thousands rejoicing and dancing before the Lord.

Some were getting out of wheelchairs and throwing away canes and joining in the dancing.

A doctor watched the cloud of God's glory pass through the camp and into the meeting hall as everyone was rejoicing in what the Lord had done.

How great and powerful is the name of Jesus!

GREATER THINGS STILL

When Jesus was on earth, He could be in only one place at a time, ministering to one person or one group of people. Once He had returned to heaven, the Spirit could be poured out on those who believed in Him. By the Spirit, the power that was in Jesus would be in His followers.

Concerning the Spirit, Jesus had made this promise to His disciples: "He lives with you and will be in you" (John 14:17). God Himself would live in them and work through them to bring the life and power of His kingdom to others.

Jesus made the amazing statement that "anyone who has faith in me will do what I have been doing" (v. 12). This is a statement of fact: *If you believe in Him, you will do the same things that He did.* It is also a promise; this is certainly what you will do if you put your faith in Him.

But He went further: "He will do even greater things than these, because I am going to the Father" (v. 12). Jesus is talking about anyone who has faith in Him, anyone who believes in His name. He is talking about *you.*

When the Spirit was given on the day of Pentecost, the original disciples became transformed men, empowered in their ministries as never before. They preached the gospel in the power of the Spirit and three thousand turned to the Lord and received the Holy Spirit themselves. It was the beginning of the "greater things than these." Such things had not happened in the earthly ministry of Jesus because it was not until He had returned to heaven and been glorified that the Spirit could come and live in those who believed.

We are living in the era of the Spirit, the times of the greater things still. There is no need for us to limit God through unbelief or to imagine His power was reserved for biblical times. All over the world greater things are happening today. The same kinds of miracles that Jesus performed are being performed now because the power of the Spirit is moving in mighty ways. Wherever there is revival, there is evidence of God's power; signs and wonders follow the proclamation of the Word. This is because wherever revival is happening, there is a great emphasis on praying with faith. People are healed in the name of Jesus because they pray expecting God to honor His words of promise.

Healing does not hinder evangelism; quite the opposite. *Wherever the healing power of God is evidently at work, people turn to Jesus in greater numbers.*

You are called to faith in the name of Jesus.
Jesus says you will do the same things He did.
Jesus says you will do greater things still.
Seeing God's power at work will give wonderful
*   evangelistic opportunities.*
Others will embrace His kingdom of power.

I tell you the truth, anyone who has faith in me will do what I have been doing (John 14:12).

53

THE CHURCH CALLED
TO HEAL

Jesus did not attempt to evangelize with a gospel of words only; He demonstrated the truth of those words by the signs and wonders He performed: "Jesus went through all the towns and villages, teaching in their synagogues, preaching the good news of the kingdom and healing every disease and sickness" (Matt. 9:35).

Jesus more than sympathized or identified with the people in their needs. *He had come not to support them in their problems but to meet their needs:* "When Jesus landed and saw a large crowd, he had compassion on them and healed their sick" (14:14).

He came as the Good Shepherd and saw healing as part of His pastoral ministry to the people: "When he saw the crowds, he had compassion on them, because they were harassed and helpless, like sheep without a shepherd" (9:36).

FAILURE OF ISRAEL'S PASTORS

One of the charges the Lord brought against the pastoral leaders, or shepherds, of Israel was that they had failed to heal the sick: "You have not strengthened the weak or healed the sick or bound up the injured" (Ezek. 34:4). This failure is one of the reasons for the Lord's being against the leaders. He promises He will come Himself and be their Shepherd; then their needs will certainly be met.

King David knew the implications of God being his personal Shepherd: "The LORD is my shepherd, I shall not be in want" (Ps. 23:1).

Before going to the cross, Jesus described Himself as the Good Shepherd who "lays down his life for the sheep" (John 10:11). He did that to enable His followers to have the full life that He came to give those who believe in Him.

He laid down His life, taking upon Himself all your sin and sickness, so that He might be *your* Pastor, *your* Good Shepherd.

To those who failed to receive His words, Jesus said, "Do not believe me unless I do what my Father does. But if I do it, even though you do not believe me, believe the miracles, that you may know and understand that the Father is in me, and I in the Father" (John 10:37–38).

Sadly, it was the Jewish pastors who opposed Jesus and tried to discredit His healings. They were jealous and fearful of the influence He was wielding over the people, who gladly accepted His healing ministry.

Similarly with the apostles, it was the Jewish leaders who opposed them and tried to prevent them from speaking and healing in the name of Jesus. The people, however, recognized that God was with the men, and many were joined to the church as the result of the healings that were taking place. God was fulfilling His promise to confirm His Word with demonstrations of His healing power.

This is what Jesus promised. This is what the Word of God declares. *When we proclaim the gospel of the kingdom, He is ready to confirm His Word with signs following.* If believers lay hands on the sick, the sick will be healed.

SENT OUT WITH POWER

Jesus sent out His disciples without any formal theological training to do the same things He had been doing. He had preached the gospel of the kingdom; He told them to go and preach the same gospel. He had healed sick people; they were to heal sick people. He had raised the dead; they were commanded to do the same. He had cleansed people with leprosy; they were also to cleanse people with leprosy. He had cast out demons; they were given authority to cast out demons. They had received freely the life, power, and authority of the kingdom; they were to go and give to others what they had received.

They could not have given what they had not received. Often the church has failed to demonstrate God's desire to heal because the pastoral leaders have not manifested the necessary faith and authority.

It should be beyond question that *He intends healing to be a normal function of pastoral leadership and a supernaturally natural part of the church's ministry.*

Clearly, Jesus gave authority to His disciples (to the Twelve and the seventy-two) to heal as well as to preach. They were to demonstrate the presence of God's kingdom among men and women in such powerful ways.

However, when commissioning the church, Jesus said to the disciples, "Therefore go and make disciples of all nations, baptizing them in the name of the Father and of the Son and of the Holy Spirit, *and teaching them to obey everything I have commanded you*" (Matt. 28:19–20, italics mine). This must include His command to heal sick people. And Jesus then promises that His presence will always be with His followers, enabling them to fulfill this commission.

Jesus challenges the faith of every Christian today when He says, "I tell you the truth, anyone who has faith in me will do what I have been doing" (John 14:12). That is His expectation of *every* believer—anyone who has faith—and this must include the ability to heal in the name of Jesus.

We do not see such things happening where there is unbelief that God will do in our day what He has clearly both promised and commanded. The church needs to repent of unbelief. God is willing to use believers today to do the same things that He did yesterday. Jesus Christ is the same yesterday, today, and forever. *God is just as willing to work today in the way He worked in the earthly ministry of Jesus.*

PASTORAL RESPONSIBILITY TO HEAL

Clearly, healing power was not limited to the apostles. Stephen, "a man full of faith and of the Holy Spirit . . . did great wonders and miraculous signs among the people" (Acts 6:5, 8). James gives clear directions to *all* Christians when they are sick. "Is any one of you sick?" he asks. *Any one* means any one. Any Christian. Any believer.

If he is sick, what should he do? "He should call the elders of the church to pray over him and anoint him with oil in the name of the Lord. And the prayer offered in faith will make the sick person well; the Lord will raise him up" (James 5:14–15).

The elders share pastoral responsibility for the congregation. *It is part of their calling to pray with faith for any in their care who are sick and anoint them in Jesus' name.*

The sick person has the responsibility to call on the elders to pray and expresses faith in so doing. The elders are to be men of faith, who give an example of faith to others. As they minister in faith to people who are sick, the Lord will give the healing.

Sadly, as the pastoral leaders of their day opposed Jesus and the early Christians when they ministered God's healing power, so many pastoral leaders do likewise today. Yet they are the ones who should be encouraging their people to believe the Word of God, to implement the commands of James, and to exercise the authority Jesus gives to all believers. How can the people be encouraged by Scripture and believe God's Word if their leaders are full of unbelief?

THE YEAST OF UNBELIEF

Jesus warns His disciples to beware of the yeast of the Pharisees and Sadducees. They were concerned with the legalistic externals of religion, with outward appearances, but they lacked hearts of faith. So they rejected Jesus' gospel of power. It was too much of a personal challenge to them.

The same is true in the church today. Only a little yeast is needed to infect the whole lump of dough. Only a little unbelief in the leadership can affect a whole congregation. Here are some typical statements that pastors make and that encourage unbelief:

- Healing is not for today.
- It is not God's purpose to heal everyone; we should not encourage people to believe they will be healed so they won't be disappointed.
- Healing is not part of my ministry.
- God will be glorified in the sickness.
- We have to accept sickness as God's will for us.

Beware of the leaven of unbelief. Take your doctrine about healing from what God says in His Word—not from the opinions of others. Beware of the leaven of those who value their own opinions more highly than God's Word; who limit Him by their rational and limited understanding; who speak against His healing power rather than fulfill their responsibilities as believers to be part of a healing church; or who, as pastoral leaders, neglect their call to strengthen weak people, heal sick people, and bind up the wounds of God's people.

It takes only a little leaven to affect the whole lump. Jesus warned the disciples against allowing even a small amount of unbelief to affect their thinking and attitudes. Holding on to tradition, putting your trust in religious practices, or believing your own opinions will do nothing to bring the supernatural power of God into your daily experience.

> *Pastors are called to heal in Jesus' name.*
> *Elders are called to pray with faith for sick people to be healed.*
> *Healing is a gift for the whole body of Christ.*
> *You are part of His body and share in His call.*
> *Beware of the leaven of unbelief.*

Heal the sick who are there and tell them, "The kingdom of God is near you" (Luke 10:9).

54

RESTORATION OF THE HEALING MINISTRY

Statements contrary to the teaching of God's Word only demonstrate the unbelief and ignorance of those who make them. We have seen how dangerous it is to create your own doctrine based on experience. The Lord wants to see faith in His church *everywhere*, so His healing ministry can be continued everywhere. This is part of the pastoral responsibility of *every* congregation and *all* who claim to be shepherds of God's people.

God raises up people with particular healing ministries, but He wants to see this ministry restored as a proper function of the body of Christ in every local congregation.

KINGDOM OF POWER

Our ability to heal in the name of Jesus verifies the truth of the gospel we proclaim: "For the kingdom of God is not a matter of talk but of power" (1 Cor. 4:20).

It is a cause for great rejoicing that during the past twenty years, many have discovered Christ's willingness to heal today. The healing ministry has been restored, or newly introduced, to thousands of congregations because their spiritual leaders have begun to exercise faith for healing. They have begun to make use of the power and authority God makes available to them as those called to exercise pastoral responsibility for His people.

All would say they are looking for greater results, but at least a start has been made. As we learn to trust the Lord more fully (or simply!) and become bolder in our faith, we shall see more fruit in this ministry, and that fruit will give glory to God.

If, as the church, we preach and proclaim a gospel of words without offering Christ's healing power, we are failing the Lord and selling His people short.

If we are proclaiming forgiveness of sins through the Cross and not the healing of sickness through that same Cross, we are proclaiming only a partial cross. If we bring people into a faith in which they have new life in Jesus but not necessarily to living faith through which they can believe God to meet needs in their lives, we are not proclaiming the whole counsel of God.

We are to expect our God to do mighty things. When the seventy-two came back, they were elated that they had been successful in fulfilling their commission. Even the demons submitted to them. Jesus pointed them to a very important truth. It was more important to rejoice that their names were written in heaven.

Jesus was not saying that deliverance and healing were unimportant. He was pointing them to the truth that they were children of His kingdom. They had seen His power at work through them because they were children of the kingdom; they belonged where demons never belong and where there is no sickness. They belonged where Satan himself was thrown out long ago.

YOU HAVE TO BEGIN SOMEWHERE

I found I had to take God's call to heal sick people seriously in the very first days of my ministry. What was the purpose of visiting sick folk? To sit by the bed chatting, exchanging pleasantries and perhaps saying a little prayer with them before leaving? That approach may have expressed some love and concern, but it was a long way from fulfilling Jesus' command to heal.

A quest began in those early days of my ministry to see how the healing power of Jesus could be brought into people's lives. What began very tentatively has gradually progressed and developed as I have grown in faith and boldness.

Now, more than twenty years later, I see thousands being healed every year. But I want to make three things clear:

1. *We all have to start at the beginning.* For me, one of the most significant moments was when I first dared to lay hands

on someone, praying that she would be healed in Jesus' name.

2. *I never stop learning about the healing ministry.* Every situation is different, and there are no great formulas. Faith is the key for me and those to whom I minister. So I need to learn how to encourage faith in others as well as be prepared to pray for them with faith.

3. *Failure always seems to dog my footsteps!* God may heal hundreds at a single meeting as the Spirit moves powerfully. But there are always those who are not healed. I could absolve myself from responsibility by saying they do not have sufficient faith, or it is not God's time for their healing. *But I know the Lord uses failure creatively in my life to urge me to seek Him for more power and greater authority in my life and ministry.*

You are a child of God's kingdom.
You have the life, you have the power, and you have the authority of that kingdom.
Begin to exercise the faith and authority if you have not already done so.
Do not allow apparent failure to discourage you. God will honor obedience to His Word.

For the kingdom of God is not a matter of talk but of power (1 Cor. 4:20).

55

EMPOWERED TO HEAL

Healing is a work of God's Holy Spirit in our lives. Jesus made this great promise to His disciples: "But you will receive power when the Holy Spirit comes on you" (Acts 1:8). If we are going to be used by God to bring healing to others, we need to be filled with the power of the Holy Spirit. Jesus gave this promise of power to explain what would happen when His followers were baptized in the Holy Spirit. This baptism is a definite event through which the power and activity of the Holy Spirit are released in the lives and experience of Christians.

POWER THROUGH GOD'S SPIRIT

To ask the Lord to baptize you in the Spirit is not a denial of any of the Spirit's previous activity in your life. It is acknowledging that you need to receive more from God, to see the presence and power of God in your life so that you can be more effective in your witness and ministry to others.

Some point to the fact that they received the Holy Spirit at the time of their conversion, when they were born again. Others say the Holy Spirit was given at their baptism, confirmation, and ordination. Nobody would want to deny that the Spirit is active in all these events or that the Holy Spirit lives within every born-again believer.

It is not what we claim that matters to God, but the

254 THE HEALING CHURCH

evidence of what is seen in our lives. "By their fruit you will recognize them," Jesus said (Matt. 7:16). If we are filled with power, there will be the demonstrations of God's power in our lives. The Holy Spirit will be able to work through us, enabling us to do the same things as Jesus—and greater things still! We will be familiar with the gifts of the Spirit in our experience, the gifts that are so vital to the exercising of a healing ministry.

MORE POWER

Nobody would question that the disciples received the Holy Spirit on the day of Pentecost. They were definitely born again and baptized in the Spirit. Yet only a short while later, we hear them praying, "Enable your servants to speak your word with great boldness. Stretch out your hand to heal and perform miraculous signs and wonders through the name of your holy servant Jesus" (Acts 4:29–30).

Although there was already ample evidence that the Spirit had anointed them to preach and heal in the name of Jesus, they were aware of their need for more power. God answered their prayer by filling them *again* with His Holy Spirit. Nobody, least of all the disciples, told God that He should not have done that because they had already received the Spirit. The Lord knew their need of greater boldness and more power—and the Holy Spirit is the answer to that need.

The same need exists throughout the church today: greater boldness and more power. It is true for us, as it was true for the early Christians, that we have a rich inheritance in Christ, that every need is already met in Him. Faith enables us to appropriate this inheritance, and the Holy Spirit gives us the ability to live in the good of it.

Those who claim that they have the fullness of the Spirit and need to receive nothing more of His power must make their words good by their deeds. Usually, those who deny the baptism of the Holy Spirit as a definite event apart from new birth argue that the gifts of the Spirit and healing are not for today. That is a convenient argument if they have received neither the gifts nor the power to heal.

The truth is that throughout the world millions of born-again believers have experienced a subsequent baptism in the Holy Spirit during recent years. This is in keeping with scriptural experience and has led to more effective witness in their lives and a definite release of power, especially power to heal people who are sick.

POWERFUL CHURCHES

In lands where vast churches are being built because of the reviving work of the Spirit, signs and wonders abound. In small groups when Christians have honestly and earnestly sought God for greater reality and more power in their spiritual lives, He has baptized them in the Holy Spirit, and they have begun to see Him work in healing power.

God is restoring the power to heal to His church today. As He prepares His bride for His coming, He wants a church as powerful as that of the apostolic age, a church familiar with the greater things still. It is time for Christians to humble themselves before God, to admit their need for greater boldness and power, to receive the Holy Spirit in such a way that will enable them to be increasingly fruitful in their witness to the world, and to meet the needs of people through the sovereign power of God.

If you recognize a lack of power in your life and ministry, ask Jesus to baptize you in the Holy Spirit. This is a promise from God that He wants to see fulfilled in all His children. Jesus described the Spirit as rivers of living water that are to flow out of your innermost being. Are those rivers flowing freely? Is there a river of power, of life and love, of joy and peace, a river of forgiveness and healing flowing out of your life to others? If not, ask God to fill you afresh with the Spirit. Humble yourself before God, acknowledge your need, and ask Him to fill you. Do not fool yourself into believing you have power if you cannot see the evidence of it in your ministry. It is by your fruit that you will be known as a disciple of Jesus.

> *Know that it is His purpose to baptize you in the Holy Spirit.*
> *When you ask, believe that you have received.*
> *Remember that He also said, "Whatever you ask for in prayer, believe that you have received it, and it will be yours" (Mark 11:24).*
> *Now thank the Lord for faithfully fulfilling His promise to you.*

Ask and it will be given to you. . . . Everyone who asks receives. . . . How much more will your Father in heaven give the Holy Spirit to those who ask him! (Luke 11:9–10, 13).

56

SPIRITUAL GIFTS

Some people misunderstand completely what Paul says in his first letter to Corinth because they think he is making a distinction between gifts and love, suggesting that there are two ways of serving the Lord, either the way of gifts or the way of love. Nothing is farther from the truth of what Paul is saying. The excellent way is the way of using the gifts of the Spirit; the most excellent way is to use the gifts in love. In chapter 12, he speaks of the gifts, in chapter 13, he talks about love, and in chapter 14, he explains how to exercise the gifts in love. The Corinthians were exercising the gifts selfishly and without love, everybody acting in independence, whereas God gives the Spirit's gifts for the common good.

If you want Him to use you to bring healing to others, you will learn to depend very much on the work of the Holy Spirit. This is not surprising because Jesus did not begin His ministry of preaching and healing until the Spirit had come upon Him. He was conceived of the Holy Spirit, yet He received that empowering for His ministry.

FIRST CORINTHIANS 12

There are several gifts of the Spirit mentioned in the New Testament. The ones mentioned in 1 Corinthians 12 are particularly relevant for ministering and receiving healing.

There is only one Spirit, but He manifests Himself in different ways. These gifts are manifestations of that one Spirit, and you will need to use these gifts in love.

We'll not attempt a full discussion of these gifts here, but we'll see briefly how they relate to the particular work of God's healing in our lives.

The word of wisdom comes as revelation from the Spirit, showing you how to minister in the particular situation in which you are placed. You will sometimes be confronted with a situation that utterly perplexes you, but the Spirit will show you what to do and say.

The word of knowledge is used in two ways in connection with healing. A person may want to be healed physically, and yet you sense that there is a deeper problem God wants to deal with that is the cause of the physical need or prevents the person from receiving healing. The Spirit is able to give you a word of knowledge as to the real need. A word of knowledge shows you what is wrong; a word of wisdom shows you how to set about praying for that need to be met.

God can also give you a word of knowledge when meeting with others, in either a small or a large group, about a particular work of healing He wants to do in someone's life. When spoken, such a word brings faith to the person or people concerned and can be the means whereby they receive their healing there and then.

Faith is a gift of the same Spirit. We have already seen how central faith is in receiving and communicating God's healing to others. Your faith has limitations, and sometimes you sense the need before you is beyond your normal field of faith. God is able to give you a gift of faith to believe the need will be met.

Similarly, He gives a gift of faith to sick people to believe they are able to receive from God. This often happens at a public meeting where healing is being offered to God's people or as the result of hearing a word of knowledge.

There are some beautiful Christians who love the Lord and are greatly used by Him but who find it difficult to believe that He acts supernaturally in their lives in answer to prayer, especially for healing. They need to seek from the Lord the gift of faith that will enable them to live at a higher level of faith than was possible before.

Gifts of healings—notice that both words are plural. There are two ways we can understand this phrase. One of the ministries God has given to His church is that of the healer, one who is particularly used by God to bring healing into other lives, using the spiritual gifts of healing. Because the gifts are for the whole church, we can also understand this phrase as referring to the particular *gifts* of *healings* received by those who were sick.

There are many ways in which God releases His healing

power into the lives of His children. Not all are healers, with a particular ministry of healing, but all are able to receive healing and be used by the Lord to further His healing purposes in others. You can obey the leading of the Spirit to lay hands on someone and see the person healed because you are a believer.

Miracles or, literally, operations of power. Some healings are miraculous in that they are instantaneous. They have occurred not through a speeding up of the natural processes of healing but through sudden and direct intervention by God. These are the more spectacular kinds of healing done in the name of Jesus, but they are not the only kinds of healing.

While many Christians do not believe that miracles are possible today and doubt that we should even pray for such things, many others are able to testify to the way in which God has miraculously intervened to heal them. Some have been revived from death, while others have experienced the miraculous working of God in ways that have nothing to do directly with healing.

Prophecy is God speaking to His children by the Spirit, and it is therefore another invaluable gift that brings healing into their lives. People can be healed as a result of prophecy because God has spoken directly into their circumstances. Prophecy is forth-telling rather than foretelling! There will be occasions when a prophetic word relates to the future, but essentially, it is a *now* word—what God wants to speak *now* into the hearts of His children. One sentence from God can bring release, freedom, and healing into a person's life It is the word she needed to hear.

When you are counseling someone, it is not hours and hours of good advice the person needs; she needs to hear from God the direct word that will unlock her situation, the word that will bring His healing power and activity into her life.

The ability to distinguish between spirits will enable you to discern whether healing or deliverance is needed, whether a person is oppressed or possessed, whether a person speaks from God or from the enemy or from himself. The Holy Spirit will give you the right witness. Sometimes you will not be able to find any logical, rational explanation for believing what you sense the Spirit is saying. You simply *know* what kind of spirit you are dealing with. You can then determine whether you need to pray for physical healing or whether you need to confront the enemy in the name of Jesus, commanding him to release the person.

Speaking in tongues (literally, kinds of tongues) is of immense value to any Christian in the prayer and praise life. Nowhere in Scripture is it referred to as the least of the gifts, and any gift from God must be good. Remember that all these gifts are manifestations of the one Holy Spirit. It makes no sense to say, therefore, that you want to be filled with the Spirit and healed but not to speak in a language God is prepared to give you supernaturally by that same Spirit.

Some hesitate to ask the Lord for this gift because they see no point in speaking words they do not understand. That is the whole point of the exercise. Because your understanding is imperfect, you need this gift. Paul said he prayed with the Spirit and with the mind also; he sang with the Spirit, and he sang with the mind also.

When you speak in a tongue, you speak to God. The Holy Spirit within you is praying to the Father, and He always knows precisely how to pray in every situation. Even though your understanding may be imperfect, the Spirit will pray in the right way. He will also pray for you, as well as in you, which is why anyone speaking in a tongue edifies himself.

When you have prayed for a person in your own language, it is good to pray also in the language of the Spirit. You may not understand, but the prayer is for God, not you, and He will understand what the Spirit says to Him. And you can be confident that the Spirit has supplemented your imperfect knowledge with His perfect understanding of the situation.

This gift, as with all the others, is always under the control of the user. So there is no need to fear that the Spirit will make you speak in tongues when you do not want to. The Lord requires your cooperation to use the gifts; He will not force you.

The interpretation of tongues. Having prayed in tongues, ask the Spirit to give you the interpretation of what has been said, for then your understanding of what is happening will increase. You will see more clearly how you are to proceed, what you are to pray, and what you need to believe. The Spirit will interpret to you what He is praying to the Father. Often the interpretation will be an ascription of praise to God, proclaiming His victory. Sometimes it will give birth to a prophetic vision or word that will fit the situation perfectly. No wonder Paul said, "I thank God that I speak in tongues more than all of you" (1 Cor. 14:18).

It would be foolish to try to use the healing power of God without taking advantage of the very tools He has made available to enable us to minister powerfully and effectively. You need to be familiar with these gifts and to use them as you have need.

Earnestly desire these gifts as God's Word commands you. These gifts are available to you if you are filled with the Spirit.

Be bold in exercising them. Even if you feel your way tentatively at first, do not allow fear to hold you back.

Use these gifts in love.

By the power of the Spirit, God will speak and act through you.

Follow the way of love and eagerly desire spiritual gifts (1 Cor. 14:1).

EPILOGUE

57

TO ENCOURAGE YOU

How have the biblical principles we have outlined actually worked in practice? The following testimonies, taken from the many letters we receive, represent a variety of ways in which people have received healing and experienced answers to prayer. Some concern major problems, others minor ones.

IN AN EMERGENCY

How would you react to a sudden crisis? A nurse wrote to tell me of what happened to her eleven-month-old baby, Sarah, who fell backward while climbing the stairs:

She literally flew through the air and landed on the floor at the bottom of the stairs on her head. I am a trained nurse and in any kind of emergency I react as one; so normally I would have rushed her off to the hospital. However this particular time, I just felt strongly that I should pray. Sarah was crying and had a huge lump on her head. I sat her on my lap and put my hand on her head where the lump was and prayed that Jesus would heal any damage that had been done. While I was praying, I felt my hand become very hot and within two minutes Sarah had stopped crying and five minutes later was playing happily. The lump on her head had gone and even a week later there is no bruising at all. There was never any question in my mind that she might not be healed. It just seemed that God told me to pray and I obeyed.

Many healings take place over a period of time. During the healing process, there may be several specific moments of particular significance, but often many people have been praying for the person. And the testing of faith that accompanies many of these healings produces perseverance.

A thirteen-year-old boy was knocked down by a car. He received a fractured skull and was paralyzed down one side. He also had a massive blood clot. His condition was so serious that the local hospital could not treat him, so he was sent to a London hospital immediately. Doctors told his mother that there was little hope for his life. She wrote,

> I want to tell you that I felt nothing at all at that news, but tremendous praise for God and I gave my son to Him at that moment saying, "Lord, do you want him now? If you do, take him; but I know you can heal."

> While we were in the ambulance I put my hands over his paralyzed body and found myself singing praises to God and also using my prayer language. I am afraid I had some funny looks from the ambulance crew.

> When the ambulance arrived my son was rushed off to the operating [room] to have the blood clot removed and I was told there was a good chance he wouldn't make it.

> As I waited while he was being X-rayed before going to the [operating room], I felt so uplifted and sang in the Spirit. I must have been alone for about three-quarters of an hour. Then two doctors appeared and said to me that they couldn't find the blood clot and there was no paralysis, but he had a very badly fractured skull and was unconscious. I was asked to stay with him as the first forty-eight hours were critical.

I sat at his bedside praising God. What a wonderful thing
He did to take away the clot and paralysis.

A week later when the mother sat by her son's bed (he was
still unconscious), she noticed he had stopped breathing. He
was resuscitated, and after a while doctors asked her whether
she wanted her child "put on a machine" or left to die.

If he was kept alive on a machine it would result in brain
damage. . . . I said to them, "God healed my son; He took
his clot away, He took his paralysis away. . . . I have seen
healing. I know God can heal. You think of something else
for treatment and I'll go and pray."

The doctors sought to relieve the pressure on the brain
while the mother went to pray:

As I walked down the long corridors I heard a very loud
voice and it said, "You have not been found wanting," and
I felt frozen to the ground.

From that day onward my son regained consciousness and
God healed him to the amazement of all. The only thing
left from the injury is his sight in one of his eyes—which
[isn't noticeable] to the onlooker.

I know that God will heal it.

Such a trial of faith may be beyond anything you have
experienced, and it shows the fruit of determination—the
willingness to persevere in faith, believing God above the
circumstances.

ANYTHING YOU ASK

Since publication of a book about how to pray with faith
entitled *Anything You Ask*, I have received scores of letters
telling of answered prayers and healings received.

A young baby had "nasty, irritating and disfiguring skin trouble." Her grandmother was reading *Anything You Ask,* and she recognized the truth of Jesus' promise—*anything* you ask! She began to pray. Then, she says, "One morning I woke up with words going round and round in my head. 'Elizabeth will be healed today.'"

The words persisted, and she asked God to confirm them with a word from Scripture. She opened her Bible to Hebrews 11:1–2: "Now faith is being sure of what we hope for and certain of what we do not see. This is what the ancients were commended for."

She was overjoyed and called her son, the child's father: "I worried at what I had done, I worried at the way I was upsetting my family, even though it was for little Elizabeth. But even so, 'Elizabeth will be healed today' still kept on and on inside me."

That evening her son called her to say Elizabeth was no better. The poor woman felt ashamed. Four days later she phoned, and her daughter-in-law tried to encourage her with the news that "the rash does seem fainter."

She continued to pray for Elizabeth and was away from home for a week. When she returned, her son phoned: "Mom, Elizabeth is clear, there's not a blemish left." *Praise the Lord—anything you ask.* Her son seemed overcome and said, "Thank you, Mom." Her answer was predictable: "Don't thank me; *thank the Lord.*"

The dear woman was surrounded by doubt, but in faith she held on to what God had said to her. Her disappointment that the rash did not disappear immediately is understandable, but it illustrates how important it is to fix one's eyes not on the symptoms but on the Lord.

A person addicted to alcohol read *Anything You Ask:*

In my darkest time I said the prayer you suggested in your book in desperation to Jesus. I'd never bothered with God at all very much and didn't really expect miracles. . . . In desperation I prayed and God answered. . . .

Today life is lovely. I love being alive. I haven't drunk for fifteen months and can cope with life as good as any. Of course there are still day-to-day problems, but knowing I have God in control I don't get as anxious as before.

KINGDOM FAITH

As part of our ministry, we distribute the Kingdom Faith Teaching Course, a series of tapes sent to individuals and groups in many different parts of the world. We send the course free of charge, and it includes a twenty-minute talk for each week, together with worksheets to refer listeners to the relevant Scripture verses. In response to the tape on healing, we have received many letters of testimony. Not all are spectacular, but they show what happens when people trust the Lord and begin to minister in simple ways to one another.

An older woman received healing through listening to this tape:

It was interesting that my [grandmother] had badly cut her leg a couple of days before we studied week 3 on the tape. So we did as the faith project encourages us to and prayed for that situation [with laying on of hands]. On the day we had prayed, just after praying, the bleeding and ooze had stopped. On the second day when we took off the bandage it was completely healed—clot and all. So we praise the Lord for His demonstration of power in answer to our prayers!

Not only does healing happen to those present; faith is released to pray for others:

We'd like to share with you something that happened when we were doing the tape on healing. Two in our group have young families and one day both the moms had taken their two-year-olds to the doctor and both were told that their children had a heart murmur. One was referred to the children's hospital, the other to the local clinic. Between this diagnosis and their appointments the following week, we had our "Kingdom Faith" meeting—it was the third one on healing, and we prayed for the two [children]. When they were taken to see their respective doctors the following week, they both received the same reply—"Why has this child been referred to me—there's absolutely nothing there to worry about." We just rejoiced together and praised the Lord!

Another letter says that a woman "who suffered with a degenerate spine and an ovarian cyst was instantaneously healed."

An Australian woman had congestion of the lungs. While she was listening to a tape of one of my meetings, she received her healing:

As I listened to the remainder of the tape, my healing came through—praise the Lord. I went to the doctor on Friday and he was speechless and confused, but announced that I was completely clear of all congestion. So I gave thanks to God.

PUBLIC MINISTRY

Hardly ever do I speak at healing services, but I do expect the Lord to confirm the preaching of His Word with signs following. That makes every meeting a healing meeting although often there is no mention of healing in the sermon. But when it comes to the ministry time toward the end of the meeting, I expect God to heal.

During the ministry time, I usually receive several words of knowledge. As they are spoken out, the healing occurs. Conditions that have persisted for years can be dramatically changed.

I receive personal testimonies of people being healed of everything from colds to cancer. Deaf ears hear and blind eyes see, to me two of the greatest of healings.

Sometimes people are even unaware that their healing has taken place at the time. A woman wrote that at the meeting she was convicted of the sin of an unforgiving spirit toward her mother, who had died four years previously. The conviction led to true penitence and "to this miraculous healing of painful arthritis at the base of my spine, which I had endured for many years." She continued,

> I was actually unaware that the healing had taken place, at
> the time; but soon after my return home I then realized that
> I was painlessly making movements that before I had
> either not been capable of, or had only achieved with pain.

The spiritual healing led to the physical healing in her case.

Often I am unaware of the healing. Even the testimonies I hear at the time are only a fraction of what God has done. It is common for me to have people tell me of the healings they received on a previous visit to their town. And sometimes they have told nobody else about it.

God made us to be healthy, and I always rejoice in the healings of young people who have been restricted from doing the things that healthy youngsters want to do. One young man wrote,

> You were given a word of knowledge by God concerning an
> athlete with an injured thigh. The Lord said He would heal
> it and that He wanted the athlete to run with Jesus.

That person was me. He did heal me and over the last few months I have run with Jesus to varying degrees. He has taught me how real He is through it, and after some training runs I have known that joy which I never experienced before I asked Christ to take hold of my life.

Four months later, he completed his first marathon.

I never cease to marvel at the sense of awe that comes upon people when they receive healing from God. I love to see their faces radiant with joy and wonder as they overflow with thanksgiving to God for what He has done.

There are a few particularly treasured moments: the privilege of someone being restored from death to life; a young woman standing before me with tears of joy streaming down her face as she said, "When I came to the meeting tonight I was blind, and now I can see"; a young boy going blind whose sight was restored; a woman healed of an incurable disease, a woman whom God used subsequently to bring healing to several others including her daughter, who was almost deaf.

It is such a great privilege to see God at work. Yet I must confess that the memory of the hundreds and thousands healed becomes a blur of happy faces and joyful praise to God. It is important not that I remember but that God is glorified. And anyone who sees Him heal knows beyond any doubt that *all* the glory goes to Him.

When we give testimony, it is important that God is not robbed of the glory that is His. I use testimonies very sparingly in my ministry, but they can have a telling effect on those who hear them. A woman with multiple sclerosis was healed after hearing of John's healing—the testimony with which this book began. She wrote,

I can now stand and work without holding on to anything (and even run to keep out of the rain!), and this week I have been able to get all my shopping from the supermarket without even thinking of taking a wheelchair—the first time for several years.

It was marvelous to be aware of His power at that meeting and I shall spend the rest of my life thanking and praising Him.

PERSONAL PRAYER

Even when praying personally with people, it is impossible to *see* the results of what is happening on most occasions. You know God's power is at work, and you sense that the person is receiving healing from Him. Once I prayed with a man at a friend's house. Four years later he wrote and told me what happened. He had been suffering from a gland tumor and had "the most spectacular healing." He said,

> I was [scheduled] for a major operation involving cutting facial muscles and nerves and freezing half my face. . . .
> The morning of the operation a [doctor] came for an examination, mislaid my [chart], and to cut a long story short, called for the surgeon—who said, "Lump gone, [chart] lost, you can go home."

Remember, many healings are gradual. So do not be discouraged if you do not experience a dramatic event.

One Kingdom Faith teaching group prayed for a seventeen-year-old girl who "had a liver infection which filled the whole body with poison." She had undergone two major operations and had been sent home from the hospital: "The doctors could do nothing for her; she was expected to die."

The group had been moved by the girl's plight, and as they prayed for her, she improved week by week. She visited her surgeon with her parents:

They were told that a miracle had taken place; she should not be alive. They had given up hope for her. Today she is going back to college. . . .

This has really strengthened our faith in Jesus' words that whatever we ask in His name He will grant it. The very truths as you say are "jumping out from the pages of Scripture" as we read God's Word.

RADIO PROGRAM

Another part of our ministry is to produce a two-hour weekly radio program during which we pray for people who phone us with healing needs. On a recent program, we had four testimonies that reflected a variety of ways in which God heals.

The first testimony was of a college student who sustained two fractures of the neck while playing football. He was healed when his fellow students prayed and laid hands on him.

A young girl was going deaf and was healed when she asked one of the elders of her fellowship to pray for her.

We played a taped interview with John telling of his healing from multiple sclerosis. (See chapter 1.)

And in the studio we had the nurse who, when on a life-support system, simply heard the Lord say to her, "By the stripes of Jesus you are healed." Against all the medical odds, she made a remarkable recovery.

In addition, a man phoned to say how his wife was healed of a long-standing back problem while we prayed for healing over the air. He did as I had suggested and laid hands on his wife's back, asking Jesus to heal her.

As you can imagine, for the rest of the program the telephone lines were jammed with people requesting prayer. We had a similar response when a medical doctor shared how he prayed with his patients and saw many miraculously healed.

We have even heard of people being healed in front of their television sets as they watched a film of one of our meetings. Though the program was filmed three months before the broadcast, God still used the word of knowledge to bring His healing into people's lives.

So many needs, so many ways in which Jesus meets them. But then He is the living Lord, who deals personally and individually with each one of us.

And now I look forward to all the letters readers of this book will write to us, praising God for the healing they have received. This is my prayer: that God will be glorified in the healing that will take place in the lives of those who read this book.

The virtue is not in the book but in Him. All I have sought to do is to allow the Holy Spirit to take God's words of truth and declare them to your heart. If He has done that for you, not only will you receive healing yourself, but He will use you to bring healing to others through your prayers and personal ministry to them.

58

HONESTY

What of people who are chronically sick? Of those disabled since birth or those who have had serious accidents that have left them with disabilities? What of those with hereditary diseases that are medically incurable? What of those with terminal sicknesses, who are given only weeks to live?

Are we to expect all such people to be healed? Of what worth are our theories about healing when confronted with such a mountain of human need? What of those born with permanent brain damage? What of older people? Should they be resigned to sickness because their bodies are wearing out?

The questions seem endless. How can we believe God's healing, rejoice that so many are set free, and yet see so much chronic sickness around us? Is God able to heal only lesser infirmities?

We lack integrity if we do not face such questions honestly. I live continually aware of these issues. Anyone ministering the healing power of Jesus is challenged by what does *not* happen as much as he is encouraged by the healings that do take place.

AS WITH SIN

What Jesus did on the cross He did for all men and women of all ages. The forgiveness He made possible covers every sin from murder to teasing. The greater the sin, the more evident the grace of God in forgiving the sinner. Murderers have met with Jesus, have known His forgiveness, and have been able to face execution confident of their heavenly inheritance.

By contrast, apparently good and upright citizens have lived in fear of death because they have no personal knowledge of the Savior.

The gravity of the sin is not the point; the point is whether the individual embraces God's answer to sin. Every man and woman is in need of Jesus.

SO WITH SICKNESS

As Jesus took all sin to the cross, so He carried every disease and sickness; He met every human need at Calvary. We can expect our sins to be forgiven and marvel at the grace of God to convert a murderer. We can expect our usual healing needs to be met and marvel when a disabled person walks, a brain tumor disappears, the dead are brought back to life.

Such things happen, and we can rejoice in them. But why are there not more such healings? It is impossible to escape the conclusion that if our faith was greater, we should see many more chronically sick and disabled people made whole.

By this I mean that if the corporate level of faith in the church was greater, we should see much more happening. I do not put the blame in any way on those who are chronically ill. The responsibility is one that all Christians share.

If Jesus has made the healing possible, it is for us as His body on earth to appropriate the blessings. There are two major reasons why we do not: one is personal, the other general.

BE HONEST WITH YOURSELF

God loves honesty and hates deception, including self-deprecation. I have learned the value of being honest with myself about what I believe and what I do not believe. I can look at people with disabilities and know what God is *able* to do. In an instant He could restore those people to perfect health. But I know I do not believe Him to do that there and then. Sometimes faith is quickened within me for such a miracle; but it is a great temptation to pray for all such people in the hope that something will happen yet without conviction that it will.

I have learned the futility of that kind of prayer. Unless faith is operating by the inspiration of the Holy Spirit, we do not see such miracles.

I can look at a body riddled with cancer and know what God is *able* to do. I can feel angry with Satan for causing such pain and grief to the Lord's people. I can exercise authority in the name of Jesus—and sometimes I know we are successful, I know we have the victory, and I know there will be a dramatic change in the circumstances—that God's truth alters the facts.

At other times I know the person is going to die. I do not see that as defeat because if the person is a Christian, she is going to pass into glory. And yet I know God's best healing purposes have not been fulfilled. Sometimes the cause is obvious; at other times one feels perplexed but more determined than ever in the fight against the devil and all his works.

Some people tell me that I should not take things so personally, that if I have prayed for someone with all the faith and authority at my command, I should be content to leave the outcome with God. But I cannot help taking these things personally. We are not praying machines but people. The Lord's chosen way of working is through the faith of His children. I praise Him for all He does through my ministry and for all the glory, for that belongs unquestionably to Him.

But I know that the only one who prevents God from working more powerfully in my life is *me*. If I trusted God more . . . If I was prepared to be bolder in faith . . . If my life was more like that of Jesus . . . If I manifested more of His authority . . .

There are no limits to faith except those we draw ourselves. As I travel the world, I see groups of people with a beautiful simplicity of faith. They have not drawn intellectual limitations within which God must work. They expect Him to be working supernaturally at every turn.

And yet I know that Jesus is the author and perfecter of our faith. I can never be content with the lack of faith in my life. I know He is able to lead me to a place of greater faith and authority.

FACING FAILURE

The first drafts of this book contained very few testimonies. In my office there are files full of letters giving testimony of the way God has healed people. There has been no shortage of material. But I did not include many testimonies for two reasons. First, I wanted to point people to the truth of what God will do in their own lives rather than to what he has already done in others. Second, my failures have made a deeper impression on me than the successes.

I rejoice whenever I see God's people healed; I inwardly grieve when I am conscious of my personal inadequacy and failure. However, I am not being negative but positive. Failure has a positive effect on my life; it spurs me on in my walk with Jesus to greater dependence on Him.

Some testimonies were later included because others impressed on me how encouraging these can be, for they illustrate the effectiveness of the teaching that is given.

Dear friend, understand this. Nobody has an effective healing ministry without love. As Paul says, what really matters is faith expressing itself in love. If we love people, we feel for them in their needs and are prepared to turn to God for answers. Our faith may not always match the need, but spurred on by love, we seek the Lord for more of His love, faith, power, and authority in our lives.

YOUR FIELD OF FAITH

A person cannot be a Christian without faith. However, the quality, the degree, and the extent of that faith will be different in each believer. Each of us has what might be called a *field of faith*. Your personal faith field has very definite limits. Anything that happens in your experience within the limitations is easy to cope with. You have no problem in believing God is able to deal with such situations. It does not matter whether it is a healing need or some other kind of problem, your instinctive reaction is, "That's fine. I know I can trust God for that." You don't have to think twice about the matter.

But some situations are definitely outside your faith limitations, outside the field of faith in which you feel comfortable and secure.

One of the first things I learned about the healing ministry was that the Lord is willing to forgive the mess, confusion, and unbelief in which He finds us as long as we are prepared to be open and honest with Him and don't try to make it appear that we believe when we don't. If you are conscious of not having faith sufficient for the need, you need to confess the sin of that and ask the Lord for a positive word of faith. You may have a personal encounter with God in prayer, or the Spirit may lead you into Scripture, bringing a message personally to your heart so that your faith may be enlarged. Then you will be able to trust God for the need that previously seemed impossible because it was outside your faith field.

When you have seen the Lord meet a need that previously seemed impossible, your faith field will be larger, its boundaries extended. If anything of a similar nature happens again, you know God is willing to provide for such a need in your life.

In due course something outside your extended faith limit arrives, and again you find yourself in the same position. Once more God will speak to you, encourage your faith by telling you to trust Him, and as you respond to His Word, so again the limitations of your faith field will be enlarged. It is only in this way that your faith and trust in the Lord increase and your faith field becomes bigger and bigger.

Sometimes we seem to take a giant step forward because of what the Spirit does within us. At other times it seems we try to believe God for enormous things when we have a tiny faith field.

CORPORATE RESPONSIBILITY

All of us need to be concerned to see God increase our faith at a personal level. But I believe the main reasons why we do not see more chronic sickness healed is because of the lack of faith, power, and authority at the corporate level within the church.

The church is called to be Christ's body here on earth, full of His power and able to meet the needs of people in His name. The church is to be the household of faith.

Sadly, as we have already observed, the church is double-minded about healing and therefore unstable in its ministry to sick and needy people. In Western civilization, they do not come flocking to churches to have their needs met. To most, the ministry of their local church is irrelevant to the meeting of their needs.

Wherever the power of God begins to be manifested, the people come. It is time for churches today to discover what Jesus and the church in New Testament times made obvious. Healing is an integral part of evangelism, and we shall be far more effective in communicating the good news of the kingdom of God when we demonstrate the presence of that kingdom with power.

I believe that in the coming years we are going to see more and more healings—and greater ones. More chronically sick people, people with disabilities, blind and deaf people will be healed. The revival that is beginning to sweep through nations is being attended by greater signs and wonders than we have so far seen.

PLEASE FORGIVE ME—AND THE CHURCH

In the meantime, I ask those with great needs to forgive me for my unbelief and for my inability to minister more of God's power into your lives. And I ask you to forgive the church corporately. We have failed you. We know our God is able to heal and wants to do so, but as yet we do not manifest enough of Him, His power, and His authority to see your needs met.

The crumb of comfort I can give you is that (and it is a mighty crumb!) if Jesus Christ is your Lord and Savior, your Healer and Provider, you can expect Him to meet with you in your present circumstances; but in the life to come you will be perfected. Gone will be the days of pain, sickness, and sorrow:

> Then will the eyes of the blind be opened
>   and the ears of the deaf unstopped.
> Then will the lame leap like a deer,
>   and the mute tongue shout for joy. . . .
> They will enter Zion with singing;
>   everlasting joy will crown their heads.
> Gladness and joy will overtake them,
>   and sorrow and sighing will flee away (Isa. 35:5–6, 10).

GOD'S SOVEREIGNTY

God is sovereign. Nothing can happen without His knowledge or permission. Therefore, some suggest, we should accept the apparent failures as God's sovereign purpose.

This is too easy, far too glib to be real. God has declared

His sovereign purpose in Jesus, and He makes that purpose known through His Word. He has declared that it is His sovereign will to heal. Wherever Jesus reigns as sovereign, the principles of God's kingdom operate, and that is the kingdom of power.

He gives His church the commission to heal as an integral part of proclaiming the gospel of His kingdom. Where Jesus reigns, sin, sickness, and death are overcome.

Yes, Jesus can reign in the one who is sick, but He also has the power to reign over the sickness.

Is it not offensive to God if we shrug our shoulders when people die prematurely of sickness, saying glibly, "It must be the sovereign will of God"?

His purpose is wholeness—health of spirit, soul, and body. I warned at the beginning of this book that we could not cover every aspect of such a vast purpose. Some seem to manifest much of the grace of Jesus in their lives without exhibiting much faith for Him to deal with the physical needs. Others can believe God readily for bodily healing without apparently manifesting too much of the fruit of the Holy Spirit.

What conclusion can be drawn from this? Simply that God is infinitely greater than any of us or all of us put together. Each of us is able to appropriate only a portion of all He has made available to us through the Cross and by the Spirit.

So the message of this book is simple: *never be content with what you have appropriated; God always has more to give you.*

And my God will meet all your needs according to his glorious riches in Christ Jesus (Phil. 4:19).

APPENDIX

FAITH-BUILDING SCRIPTURES

You can use the following verses of Scripture in meditation and prayer. Hear the Lord speak them to your heart by the Spirit.

CONCERNING GOD'S NATURE

Praise be to the God and Father of our Lord Jesus Christ, the Father of compassion and the God of all comfort, who comforts us in all our troubles (2 Cor. 1:3–4).

The Lord is full of compassion and mercy (James 5:11).

The Lord is gracious and compassionate,
    slow to anger and rich in love.
The Lord is good to all;
    he has compassion on all he has made (Ps. 145:8–9).

The Lord is my rock, my fortress and my deliverer (Ps. 18:2).

Is anything too hard for the Lord? (Gen. 18:14).

The Lord is faithful to all his promises
    and loving toward all he has made (Ps. 145:13).

Cast all your anxiety on him because he cares for you (1 Pet. 5:7).

The Lord is my shepherd, I shall not be in want (Ps. 23:1).

And God is able to make all grace abound to you, so that in all things at all times, having all that you need, you will abound in every good work (2 Cor. 9:8).

I am the LORD, who heals you (Exod. 15:26).

JESUS' HEALING MINISTRY

For I have come down from heaven not to do my will but to do the will of him who sent me (John 6:38).

He has sent me to proclaim freedom for the prisoners and recovery of sight for the blind, to release the oppressed, to proclaim the year of the Lord's favor (Luke 4:18–19).

Jesus went throughout Galilee, teaching in their synagogues, preaching the good news of the kingdom, and healing every disease and sickness among the people (Matt. 4:23).

When evening came, many who were demon-possessed were brought to him, and he drove out the spirits with a word and healed all the sick. This was to fulfill what was spoken through the prophet Isaiah: "He took up our infirmities and carried our diseases" (Matt. 8:16–17).

News about him spread all over Syria, and people brought to him all who were ill with various diseases, those suffering severe pain, the demon-possessed, those having seizures, and the paralyzed, and he healed them (Matt. 4:24).

When Jesus landed and saw a large crowd, he had compassion on them and healed their sick (Matt. 14:14).

I have come that they may have life, and have it to the full (John 10:10).

The Spirit of the Sovereign LORD is on me,
because the LORD has anointed me

to preach good news to the poor. . . .
To proclaim the year of the LORD's favor
    and the day of vengeance of our God,
to comfort all who mourn,
    and provide for those who grieve in Zion—
to bestow on them a crown of beauty
    instead of ashes,
the oil of gladness
    instead of mourning,
and a garment of praise
    instead of a spirit of despair (Isa. 61:1–3).

THE CROSS

Surely he took up our infirmities
    and carried our sorrows,
yet we considered him stricken by God,
    smitten by him, and afflicted.
But he was pierced for our transgressions,
    he was crushed for our iniquities;
the punishment that brought us peace
        was upon him,
    and by his wounds we are healed (Isa. 53:4–5).

For you know the grace of our Lord Jesus Christ, that though he was rich, yet for your sakes he became poor, so that you through his poverty might become rich (2 Cor. 8:9).

Whenever you eat this bread and drink this cup, you proclaim the Lord's death until he comes (1 Cor. 11:26).

[He] forgives all your sins and heals all your diseases (Ps. 103:3).

It is for freedom that Christ has set us free (Gal. 5:1).

If the Son sets you free, you will be free indeed (John 8:36).

PRAYER PROMISES

Call upon me in the day of trouble;
 I will deliver you, and you will honor me (Ps. 50:15).

Ask and it will be given to you.... Everyone who asks receives (Luke 11:9–10).

And I will do whatever you ask in my name, so that the Son may bring glory to the Father (John 14:13).

You may ask me for anything in my name, and I will do it (John 14:14).

You did not choose me, but I chose you and appointed you to go and bear fruit—fruit that will last. Then the Father will give you whatever you ask in my name (John 15:16).

I tell you the truth, my Father will give you whatever you ask in my name. Until now you have not asked for anything in my name. Ask and you will receive, and your joy will be complete (John 16:23–24).

Therefore I tell you, whatever you ask for in prayer, believe that you have received it, and it will be yours (Mark 11:24).

If you believe, you will receive whatever you ask for in prayer (Matt. 21:22).

Again, I tell you that if two of you on earth agree about anything you ask for, it will be done for you by my Father in heaven. For where two or three come together in my name, there am I with them (Matt. 18:19–20).

And my God will meet all your needs according to his glorious riches in Christ Jesus (Phil. 4:19).

He who raised Christ from the dead will also give life to your mortal bodies through his Spirit, who lives in you (Rom. 8:11).

Give, and it will be given to you. A good measure, pressed down, shaken together and running over, will be poured into your lap. For with the measure you use, it will be measured to you (Luke 6:38).

I will take away sickness from among you, and none will miscarry or be barren in your land. I will give you a full life span (Exod. 23:25–26).

APPROACH GOD IN PRAYER

Be joyful always; pray continually; give thanks in all circumstances, for this is God's will for you in Christ Jesus (1 Thess. 5:16–18).

Rejoice in the Lord always. I will say it again: Rejoice! Let your gentleness be evident to all. The Lord is near. Do not be anxious about anything, but in everything, by prayer and petition, with thanksgiving, present your requests to God. And the peace of God, which transcends all understanding, will guard your hearts and minds in Christ Jesus (Phil. 4:4–7).

And when you stand praying, if you hold anything against anyone, forgive him, so that your Father in heaven may forgive you your sins (Mark 11:25).

If you forgive men when they sin against you, your heavenly Father will also forgive you (Matt. 6:14).

Dear friends, if our hearts do not condemn us, we have confidence before God and receive from him anything we ask, because we obey his commands and do what pleases him (1 John 3:21–22).

Delight yourself in the LORD
　and he will give you the desires of your heart (Ps. 37:4).

Let us then approach the throne of grace with confidence, so that we may receive mercy and find grace to help us in our time of need (Heb. 4:16).

Let us draw near to God with a sincere heart in full assurance of faith (Heb. 10:22).

The prayer of a righteous man is powerful and effective (James 5:16).

THE WORD

My son, pay attention to what I say;
    listen closely to my words.
Do not let them out of your sight,
    keep them within your heart;
for they are life to those who find them
    and health to a man's whole body.
Above all else, guard your heart,
    for it is the wellspring of life (Prov. 4:20–23).

He sent forth his word and healed them (Ps. 107:20).

If you hold to my teaching, you are really my disciples. Then you will know the truth, and the truth will set you free (John 8:31–32).

So is my word that goes out from my mouth:
    It will not return to me empty,
but will accomplish what I desire
    and achieve the purpose for which I sent it (Isa. 55:11).

FAITH

Just say the word, and my servant will be healed (Matt. 8:8).

The prayer offered in faith will make the sick person well (James 5:15).

Have faith in God (Mark 11:22).

I do believe; help me overcome my unbelief! (Mark 9:24).

Let us fix our eyes on Jesus, the author and perfecter of our faith (Heb. 12:2).

Trust in the LORD with all your heart
and lean not on your own understanding (Prov. 3:5).

The only thing that counts is faith expressing itself through love (Gal. 5:6).

He [Abraham] did not waver through unbelief regarding the promise of God, but was strengthened in his faith and gave glory to God, being fully persuaded that God had power to do what he had promised (Rom. 4:20–21).

We do not want you to become lazy, but to imitate those who through faith and patience inherit what has been promised (Heb. 6:12).

Faith is being sure of what we hope for and certain of what we do not see (Heb. 11:1).

If I only touch his cloak, I will be healed (Matt. 9:21).

They begged him to let them touch even the edge of his cloak, and all who touched him were healed (Mark 6:56).

By faith in the name of Jesus, this man whom you see and know was made strong. It is Jesus' name and the faith that comes through him that has given this complete healing to him, as you can all see (Acts 3:16).

It is by the name of Jesus Christ of Nazareth, whom you crucified but whom God raised from the dead, that this man stands before you healed (Acts 4:10).

I tell you the truth, if you have faith as small as a mustard seed, you can say to this mountain, "Move from here to there" and it will move. Nothing will be impossible for you (Matt. 17:20).

Don't be afraid; just believe (Mark 5:36).

JESUS' WORDS OF HEALING

Take heart, son; your sins are forgiven (Matt. 9:2).

I am willing. . . . Be clean! (Matt. 8:3).

Daughter, your faith has healed you. Go in peace and be freed from your suffering (Mark 5:34).

Go . . . your faith has healed you (Mark 10:52).

Everything is possible for him who believes (Mark 9:23).

ANSWERED PRAYER

O Lord my God, I called to you for help
  and you healed me (Ps. 30:2).

Peace I leave with you; my peace I give you. I do not give to you as the world gives. Do not let your hearts be troubled and do not be afraid (John 14:27).

Dear friend, I pray that you may enjoy good health and that all may go well with you, even as your soul is getting along well (3 John 2).

Praise the Lord, O my soul;
  all my inmost being, praise his holy name.
Praise the Lord, O my soul,
  and forget not all his benefits (Ps. 103:1–2).

From the fullness of his grace we have all received one blessing after another (John 1:16).

LIVING IN CHRIST

It is because of him [God] that you are in Christ Jesus (1 Cor. 1:30).

Remain in me, and I will remain in you (John 15:4).

If you remain in me and my words remain in you, ask whatever you wish, and it will be given you (John 15:7).

We know that we live in him and he in us, because he has given us of his Spirit (1 John 4:13).

If anyone acknowledges that Jesus is the Son of God, God lives in him and he in God (1 John 4:15).

But now in Christ Jesus you who once were far away have been brought near through the blood of Christ (Eph. 2:13).

If anyone is in Christ, he is a new creation; the old has gone, the new has come! (2 Cor. 5:17).

You died, and your life is now hidden with Christ in God (Col. 3:3).

But you were washed, you were sanctified, you were justified in the name of the Lord Jesus Christ and by the Spirit of our God (1 Cor. 6:11).

So then, just as you received Christ Jesus as Lord, continue to live in him, rooted and built up in him, strengthened in the faith as you were taught, and overflowing with thankfulness (Col. 2:6–7).

Be transformed by the renewing of your mind. Then you will be able to test and approve what God's will is—his good, pleasing and perfect will (Rom. 12:2).

We take captive every thought to make it obedient to Christ (2 Cor. 10:5).

KINGDOM POWER AND AUTHORITY

The kingdom of God is near. Repent and believe the good news! (Mark 1:15).

The kingdom of God is not a matter of talk but of power (1 Cor. 4:20).

But seek first his kingdom and his righteousness, and all these things will be given to you as well (Matt. 6:33).

The kingdom of God is within you (Luke 17:21).

You will receive power when the Holy Spirit comes on you (Acts 1:8).

The one who is in you is greater than the one who is in the world (1 John 4:4).

OUR COMMISSION TO HEAL

Heal the sick who are there and tell them, "The kingdom of God is near you" (Luke 10:9).

When Jesus had called the Twelve together, he gave them power and authority to drive out all demons and to cure diseases, and he sent them out to preach the kingdom of God and to heal the sick (Luke 9:1–2).

I have given you authority to trample on snakes and scorpions and to overcome all the power of the enemy; nothing will harm you (Luke 10:19).

I tell you the truth, whatever you bind on earth will be bound in heaven, and whatever you loose on earth will be loosed in heaven (Matt. 18:18).

And these signs will accompany those who believe: In my name they will drive out demons;. . . they will place their hands on sick people, and they will get well (Mark 16:17–18).

Anyone who has faith in me will do what I have been doing. He will do even greater things than these, because I am going to the Father (John 14:12).

They drove out many demons and anointed many sick people with oil and healed them (Mark 6:13).

In the name of Jesus Christ of Nazareth, walk (Acts 3:6).

Enable your servants to speak your word with great boldness. Stretch out your hand to heal and perform miraculous signs and wonders through the name of your holy servant Jesus (Acts 4:29–30).

For God did not give us a spirit of timidity, but a spirit of power, of love and of self-discipline (2 Tim. 1:7).

Therefore confess your sins to each other and pray for each other so that you may be healed (James 5:16).

Thanks be to God! He gives us the victory through our Lord Jesus Christ (1 Cor. 15:57).